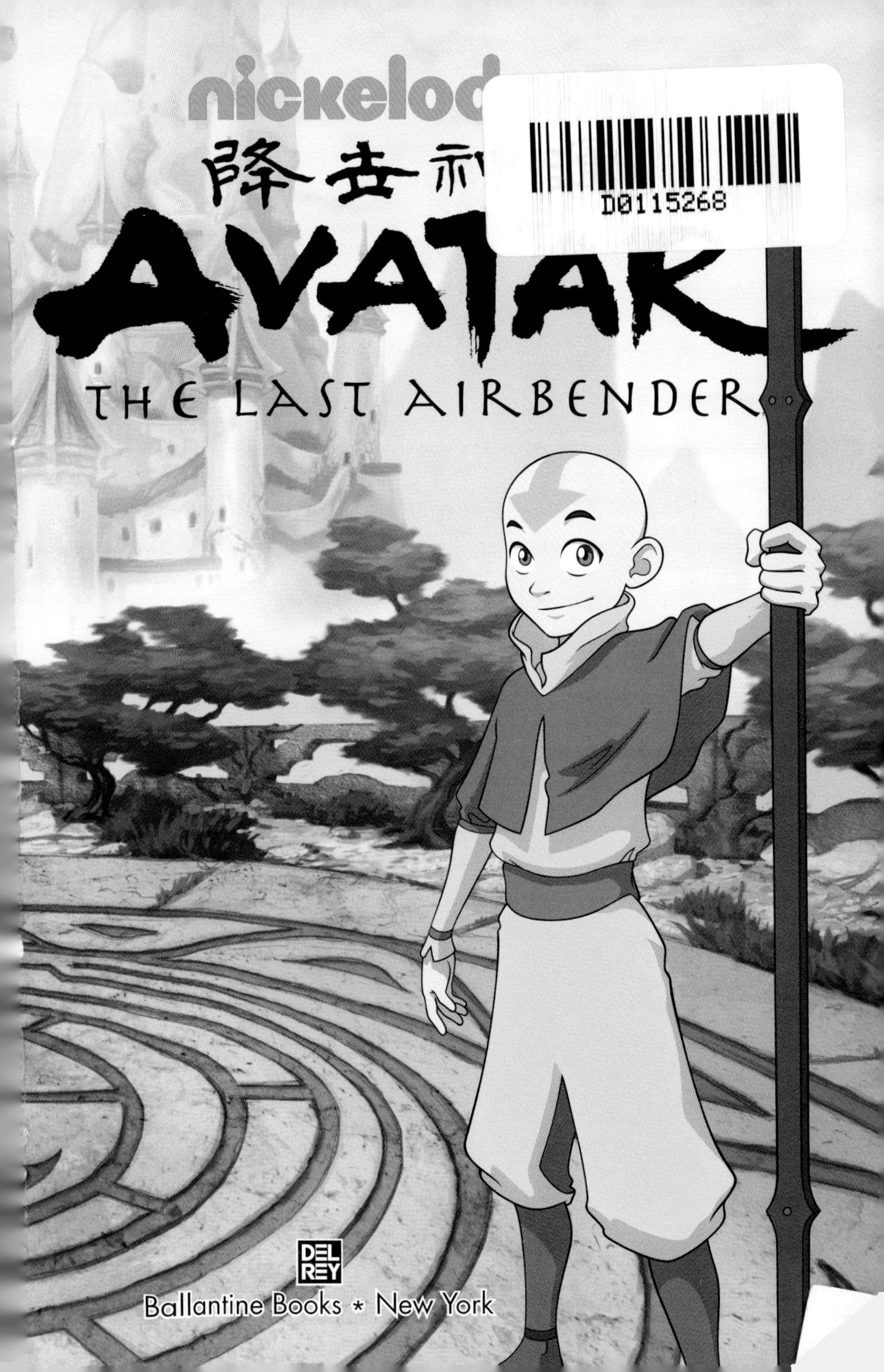
nickelod
降去
AVATAR
THE LAST AIRBENDER
DEL REY
Ballantine Books * New York

Avatar: The Last Airbender volume 1 is a work of fiction. Names, characters, places, and incidents are the products of the authors' imaginations or are used fictitiously. Any resemblance to actual events, locales, or persons, living or dead, is entirely coincidental.

A Del Rey Manga Trade Paperback Edition

Published in the United States by Del Rey, an imprint of The Random House Publishing Group, a division of Random House, Inc., New York.

Del Rey is a registered trademark and the Del Rey colophon is a trademark of Random House, Inc.

Originally published in 2006 by TokyoPop.

ISBN 978-0-345-51852-1

Printed in the United States of America

www.delreymanga.com

9 8 7 6 5 4 3 2 1

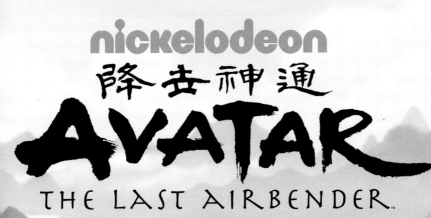

nickelodeon

降世神通

AVATAR

THE LAST AIRBENDER™

Created by
Michael Dante DiMartino
& Bryan Konietzko

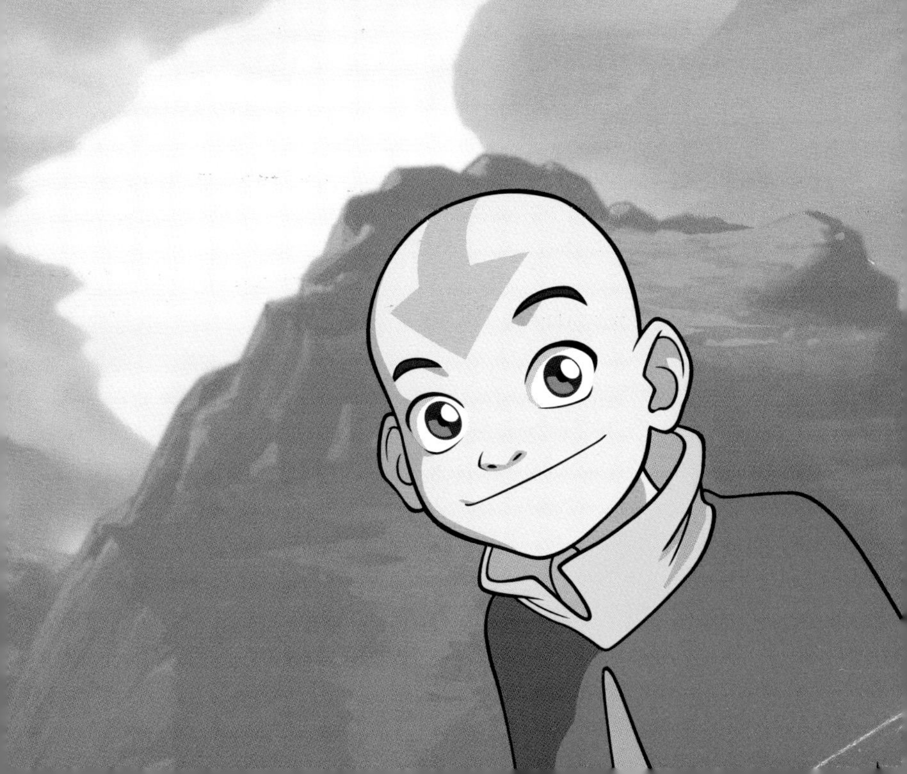

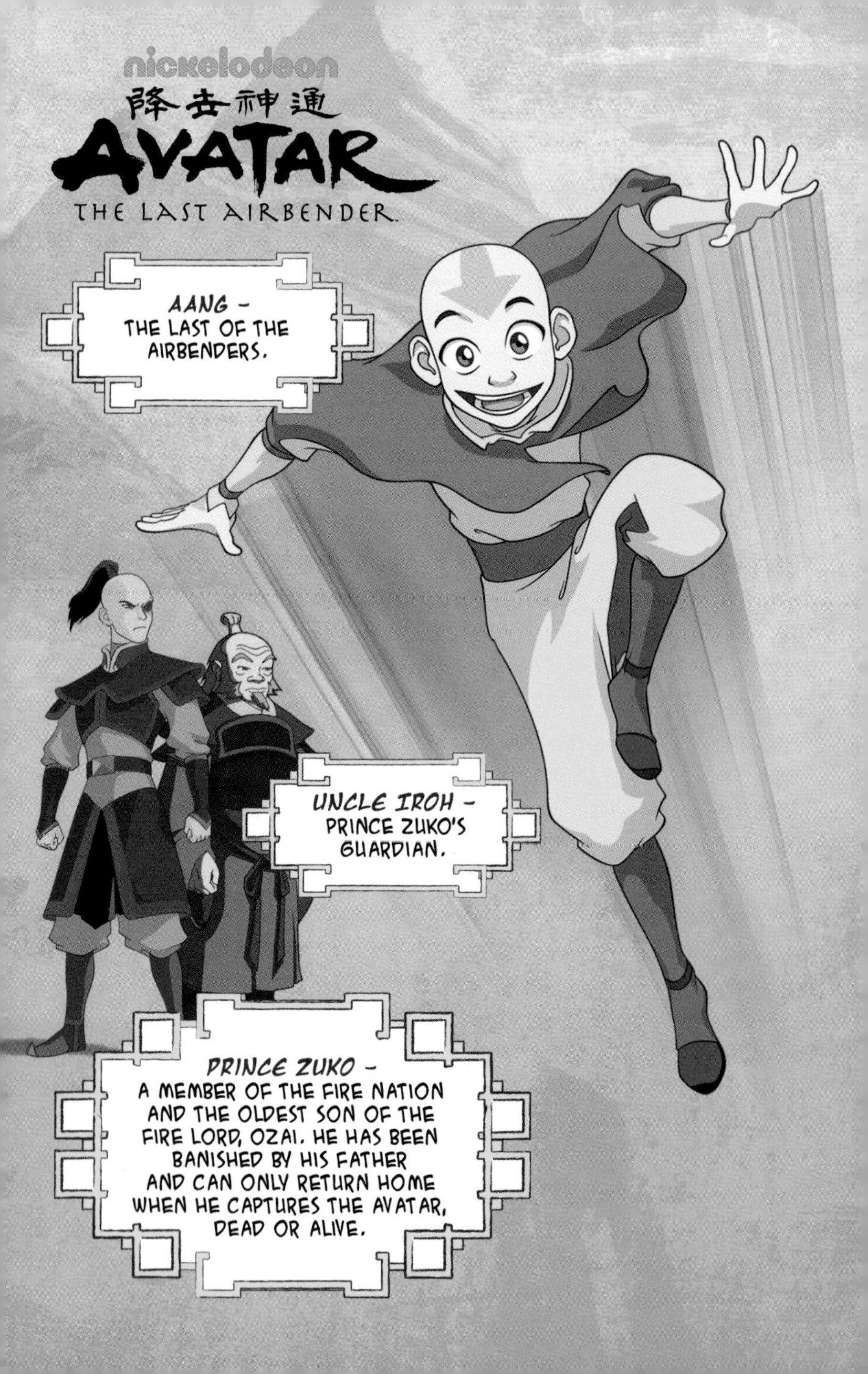
nickelodeon
降世神通
AVATAR
THE LAST AIRBENDER
AANG – THE LAST OF THE AIRBENDERS.
UNCLE IROH – PRINCE ZUKO'S GUARDIAN.
PRINCE ZUKO – A MEMBER OF THE FIRE NATION AND THE OLDEST SON OF THE FIRE LORD, OZAI. HE HAS BEEN BANISHED BY HIS FATHER AND CAN ONLY RETURN HOME WHEN HE CAPTURES THE AVATAR, DEAD OR ALIVE.

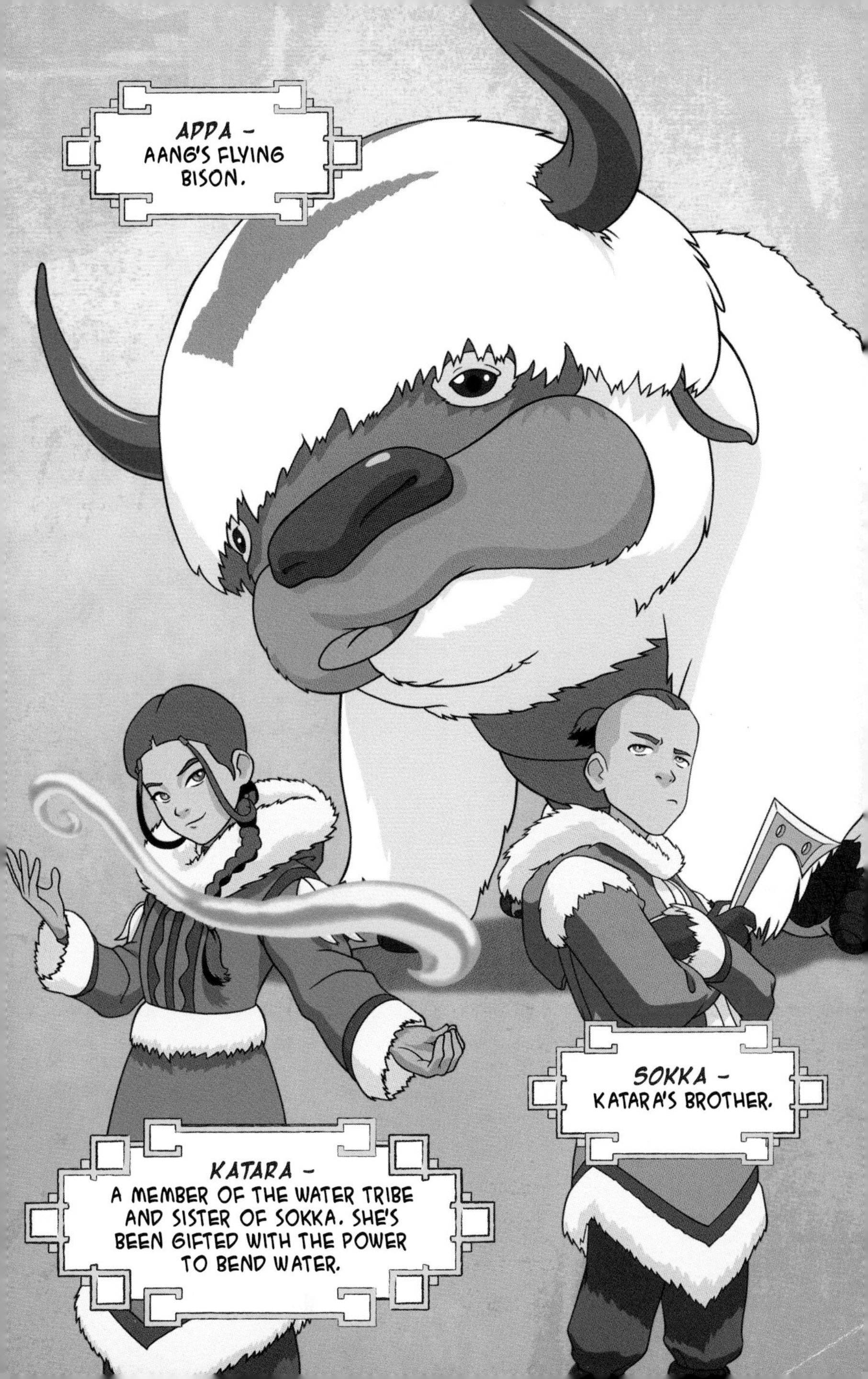
APPA – AANG'S FLYING BISON.
KATARA – A MEMBER OF THE WATER TRIBE AND SISTER OF SOKKA. SHE'S BEEN GIFTED WITH THE POWER TO BEND WATER.
SOKKA – KATARA'S BROTHER.

nickelodeon

降击神通

AVATAR

THE LAST AIRBENDER.

VOL. 1 CONTENTS

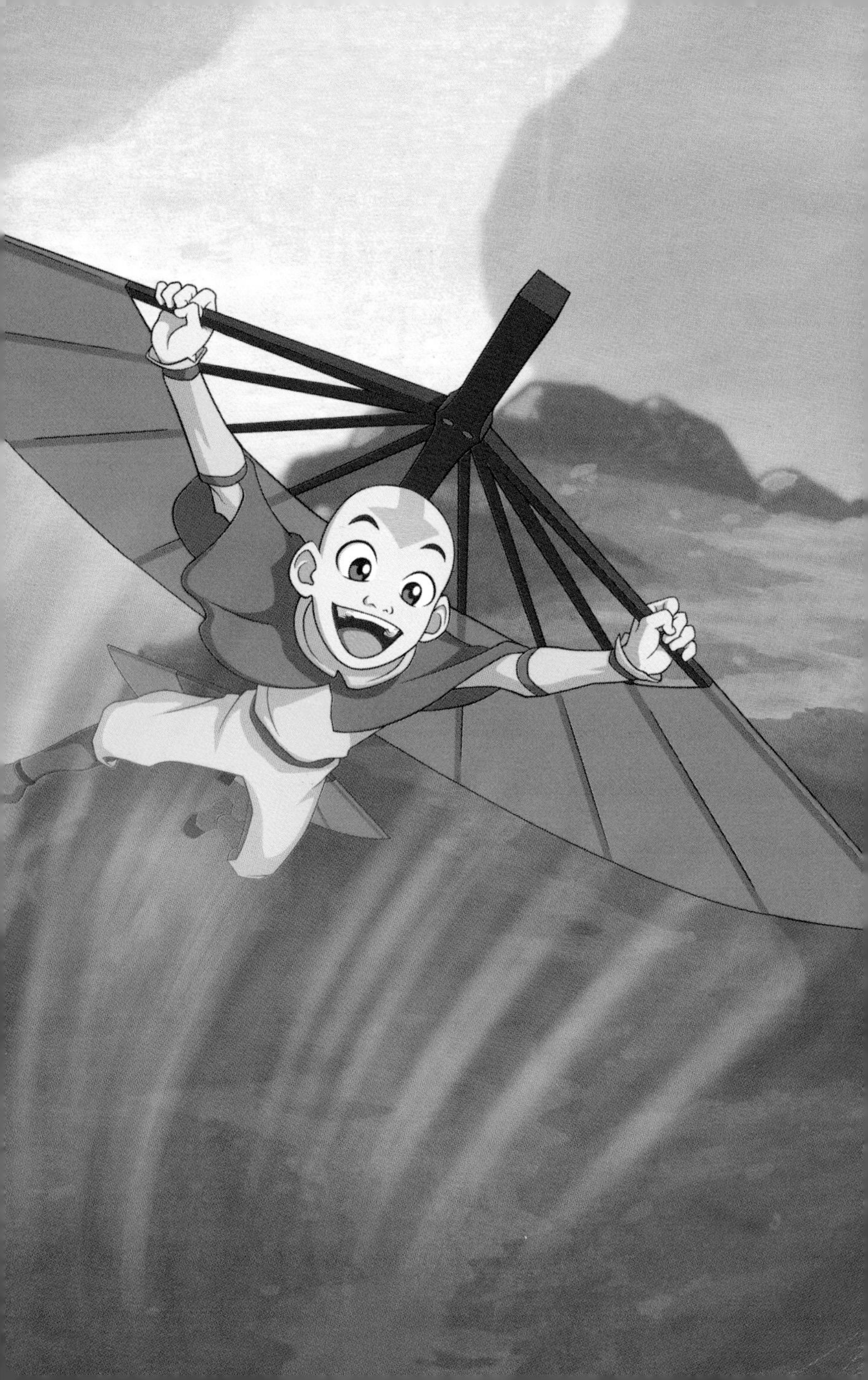

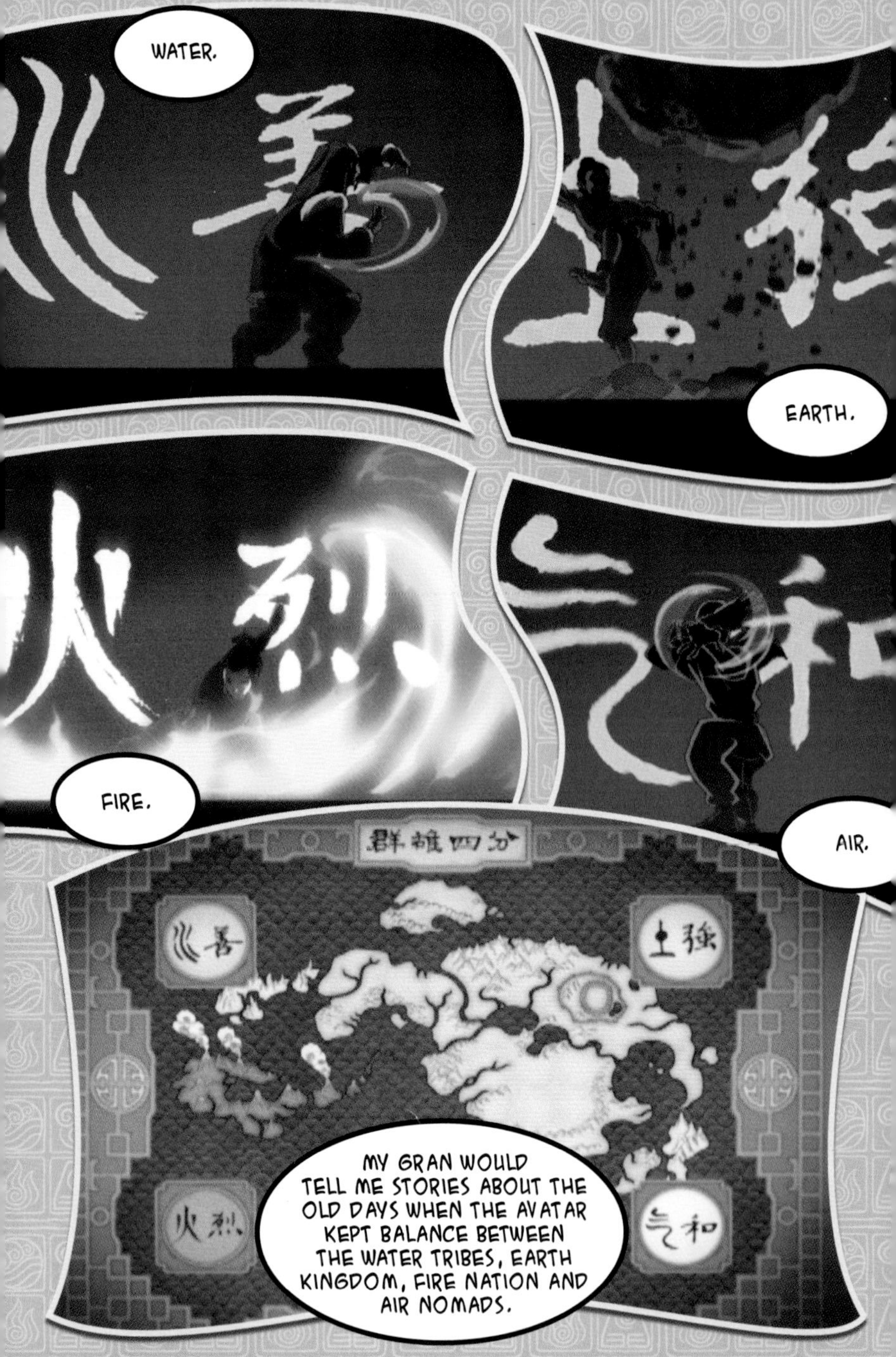
WATER.
EARTH.
FIRE.
AIR.
MY GRAN WOULD TELL ME STORIES ABOUT THE OLD DAYS WHEN THE AVATAR KEPT BALANCE BETWEEN THE WATER TRIBES, EARTH KINGDOM, FIRE NATION AND AIR NOMADS.

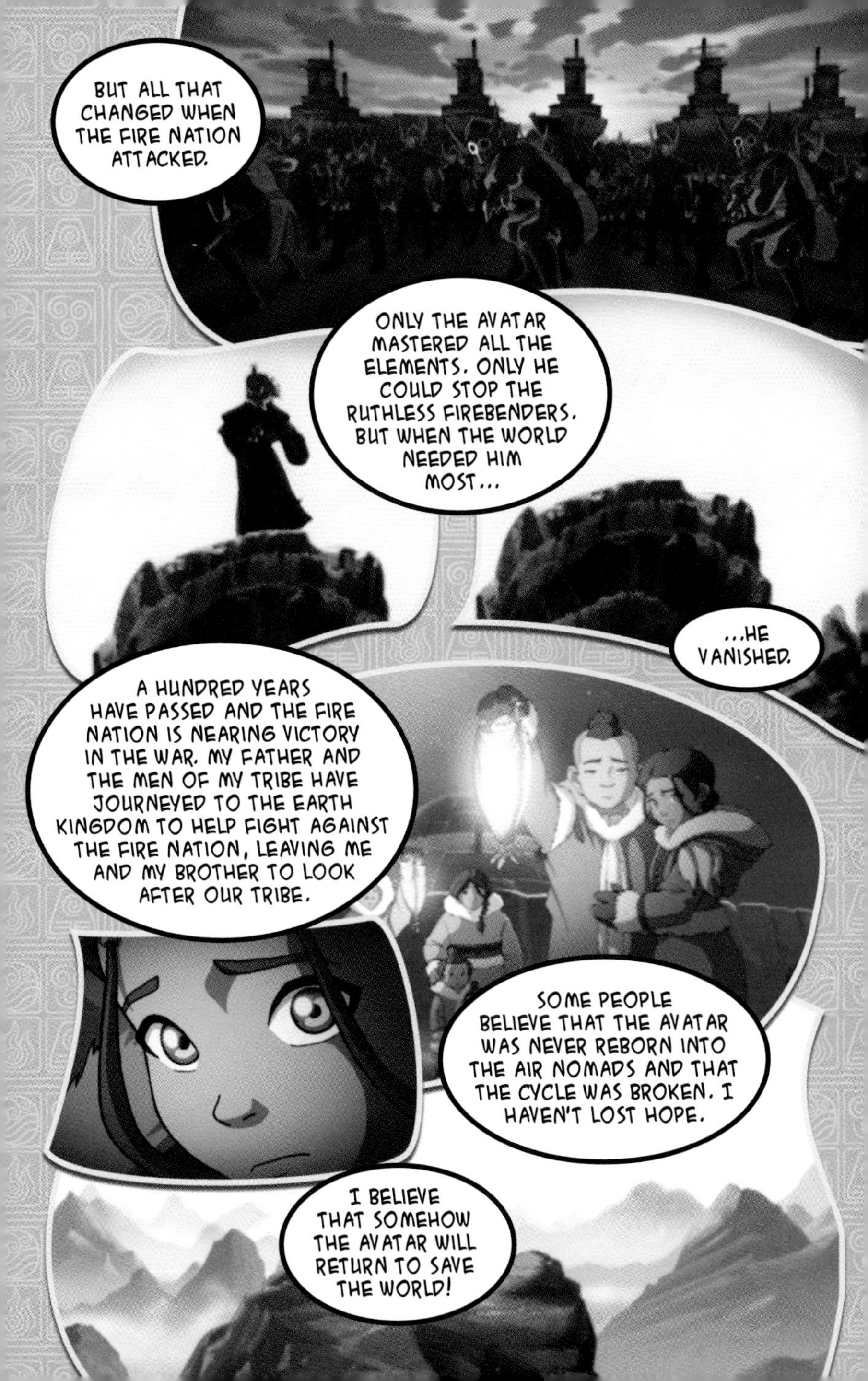
BUT ALL THAT CHANGED WHEN THE FIRE NATION ATTACKED.
ONLY THE AVATAR MASTERED ALL THE ELEMENTS. ONLY HE COULD STOP THE RUTHLESS FIREBENDERS. BUT WHEN THE WORLD NEEDED HIM MOST...
...HE VANISHED.
A HUNDRED YEARS HAVE PASSED AND THE FIRE NATION IS NEARING VICTORY IN THE WAR. MY FATHER AND THE MEN OF MY TRIBE HAVE JOURNEYED TO THE EARTH KINGDOM TO HELP FIGHT AGAINST THE FIRE NATION, LEAVING ME AND MY BROTHER TO LOOK AFTER OUR TRIBE.
SOME PEOPLE BELIEVE THAT THE AVATAR WAS NEVER REBORN INTO THE AIR NOMADS AND THAT THE CYCLE WAS BROKEN. I HAVEN'T LOST HOPE.
I BELIEVE THAT SOMEHOW THE AVATAR WILL RETURN TO SAVE THE WORLD!

BOOK ONE: WATER

THE BOY IN THE ICEBERG

WRITTEN BY
MICHAEL DANTE DIMARTINO
& BRYAN KONIETZKO

ADDITIONAL WRITING BY
AARON EHASZ, PETER GOLDFINGER,
& JOSH STOLBERG

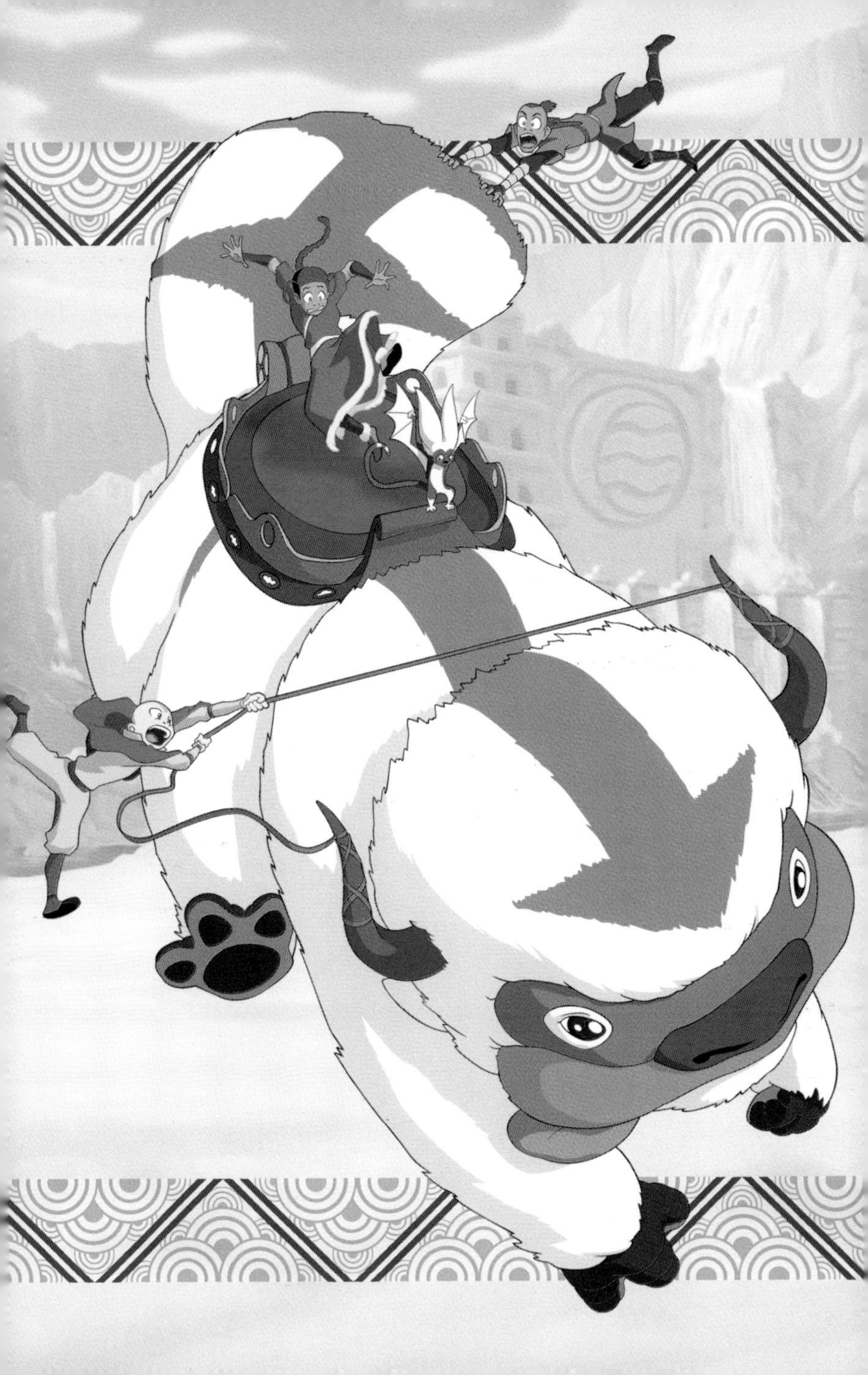

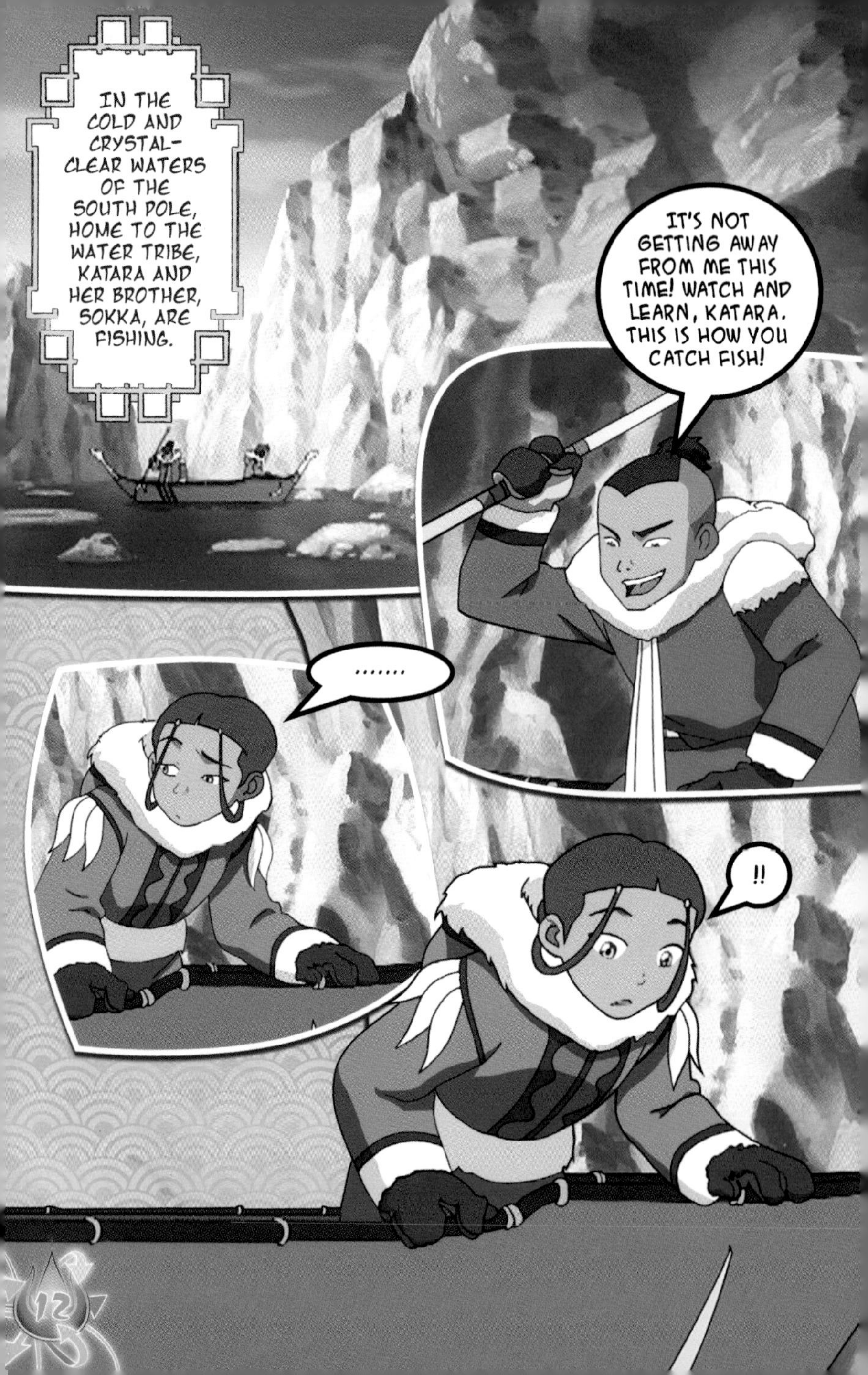
IN THE COLD AND CRYSTAL-CLEAR WATERS OF THE SOUTH POLE, HOME TO THE WATER TRIBE, KATARA AND HER BROTHER, SOKKA, ARE FISHING.
IT'S NOT GETTING AWAY FROM ME THIS TIME! WATCH AND LEARN, KATARA. THIS IS HOW YOU CATCH FISH!
....
!!

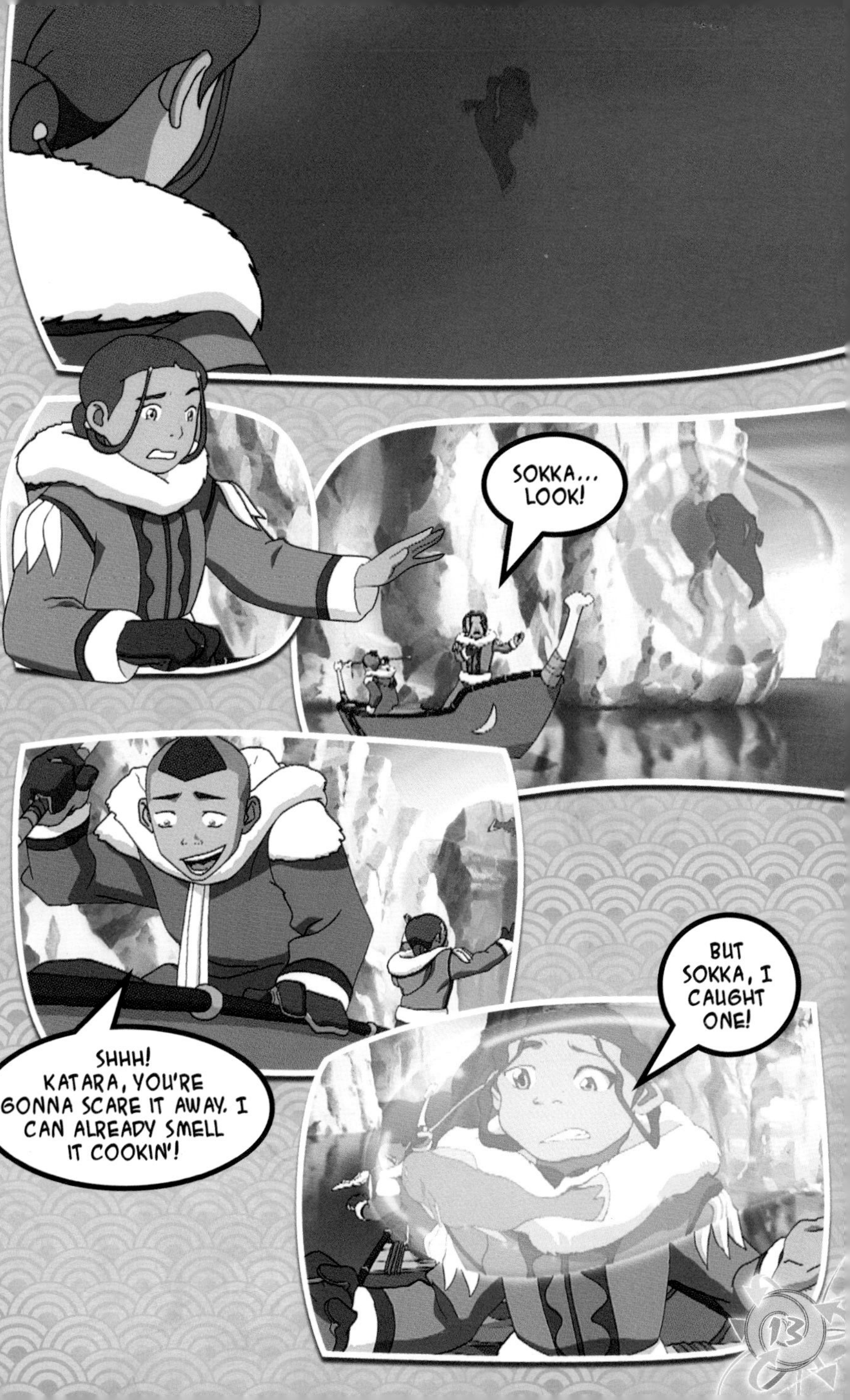
SOKKA... LOOK!
SHHH! KATARA, YOU'RE GONNA SCARE IT AWAY. I CAN ALREADY SMELL IT COOKIN'!
BUT SOKKA, I CAUGHT ONE!
13

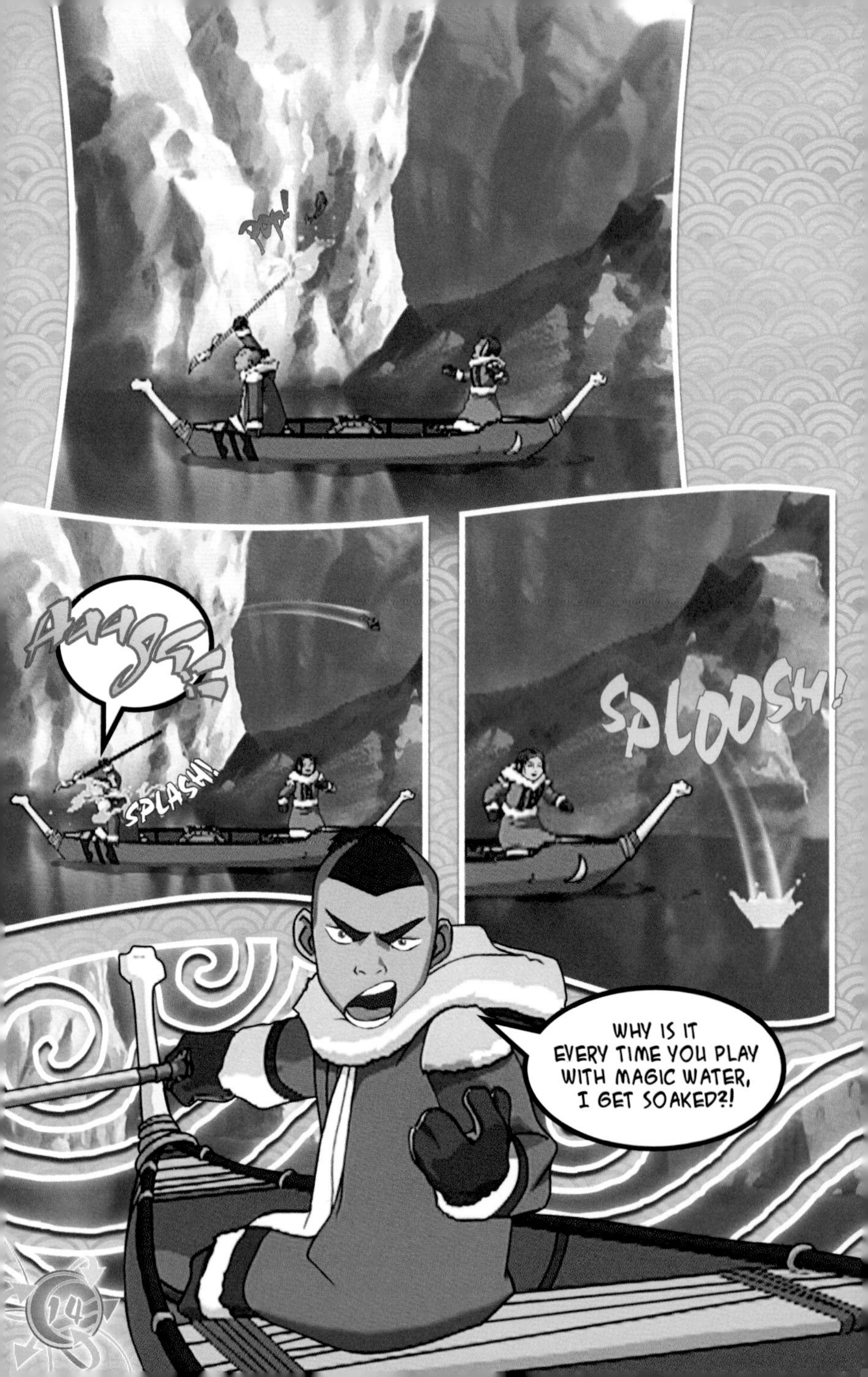
POP!
AAAGH!!
SPLASH!
SPLOOSH!
WHY IS IT EVERY TIME YOU PLAY WITH MAGIC WATER, I GET SOAKED?!

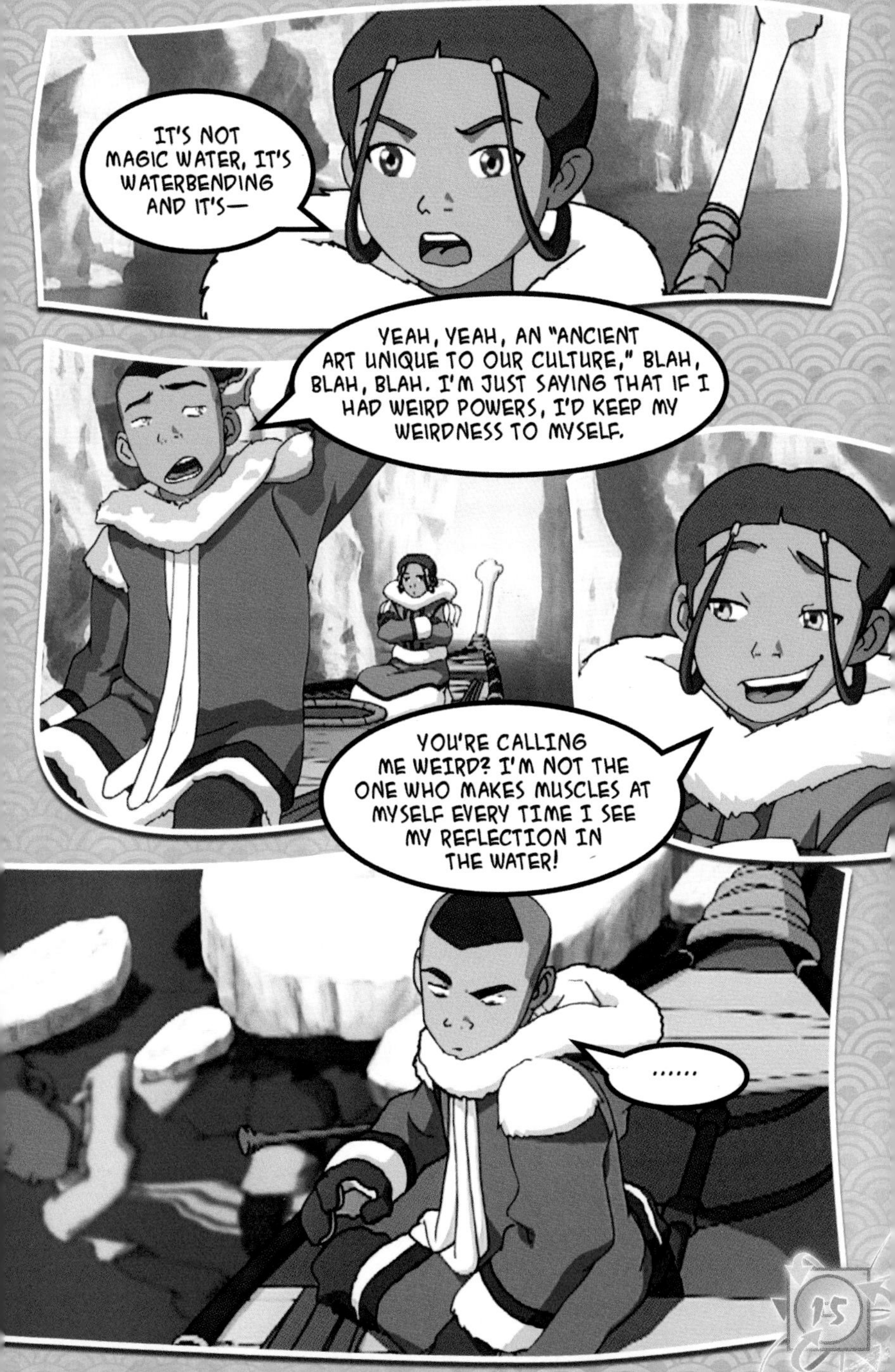
IT'S NOT MAGIC WATER, IT'S WATERBENDING AND IT'S—
YEAH, YEAH, AN "ANCIENT ART UNIQUE TO OUR CULTURE," BLAH, BLAH, BLAH. I'M JUST SAYING THAT IF I HAD WEIRD POWERS, I'D KEEP MY WEIRDNESS TO MYSELF.
YOU'RE CALLING ME WEIRD? I'M NOT THE ONE WHO MAKES MUSCLES AT MYSELF EVERY TIME I SEE MY REFLECTION IN THE WATER!
......

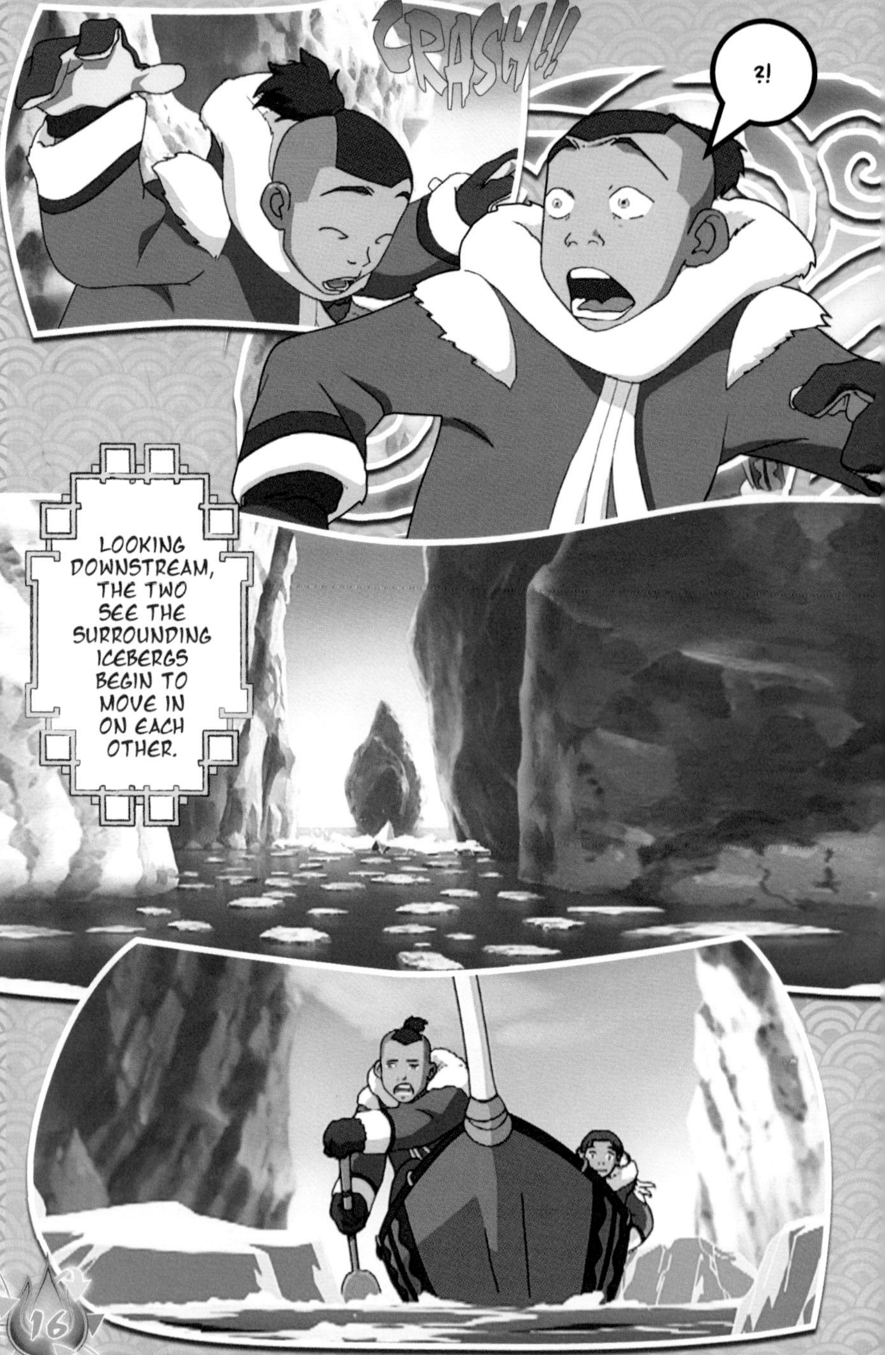
CRASH!!
?!
LOOKING DOWNSTREAM, THE TWO SEE THE SURROUNDING ICEBERGS BEGIN TO MOVE IN ON EACH OTHER.

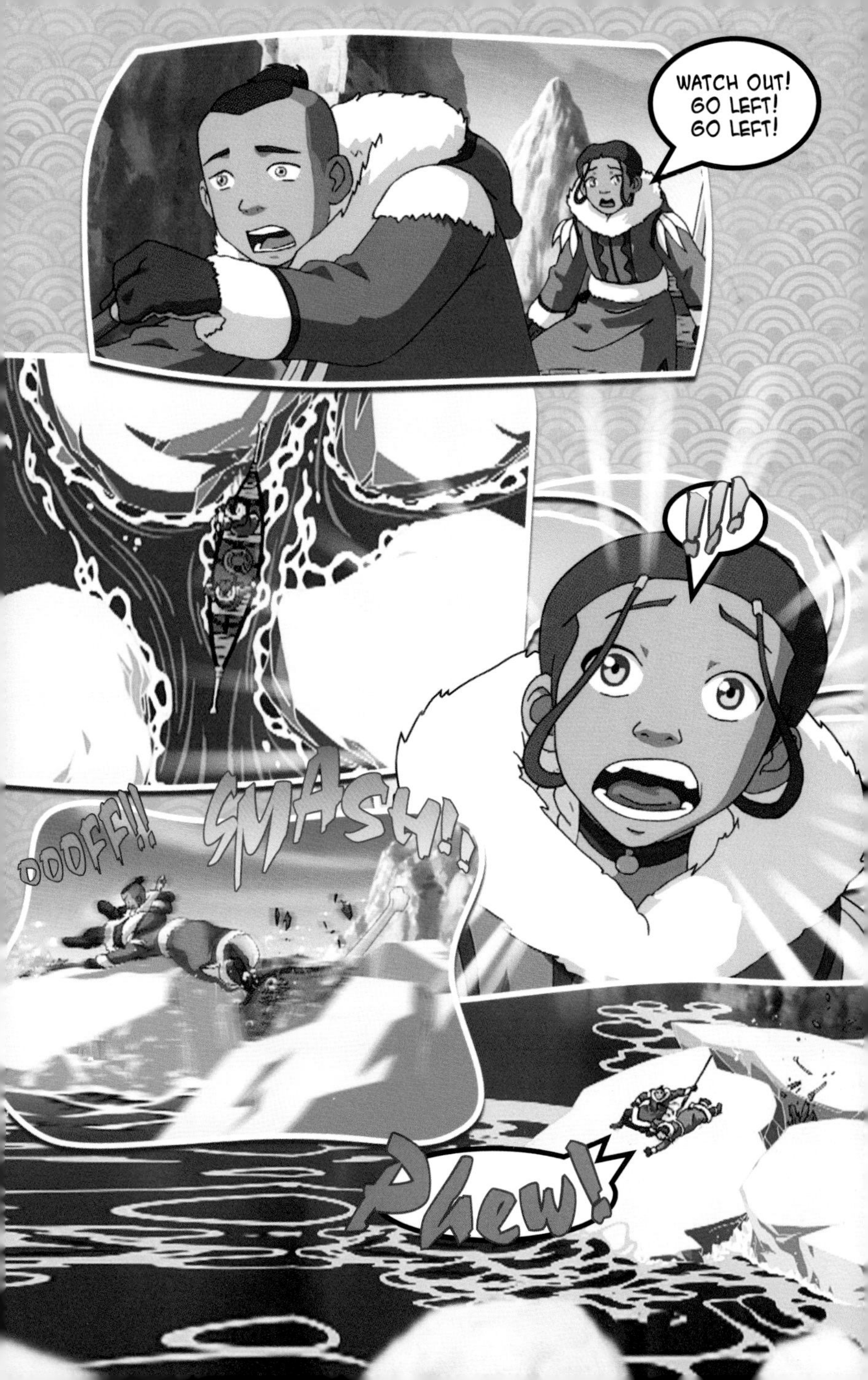

WATCH OUT! GO LEFT! GO LEFT!
!!
OOOFF!!
SMASH!!
Phew!

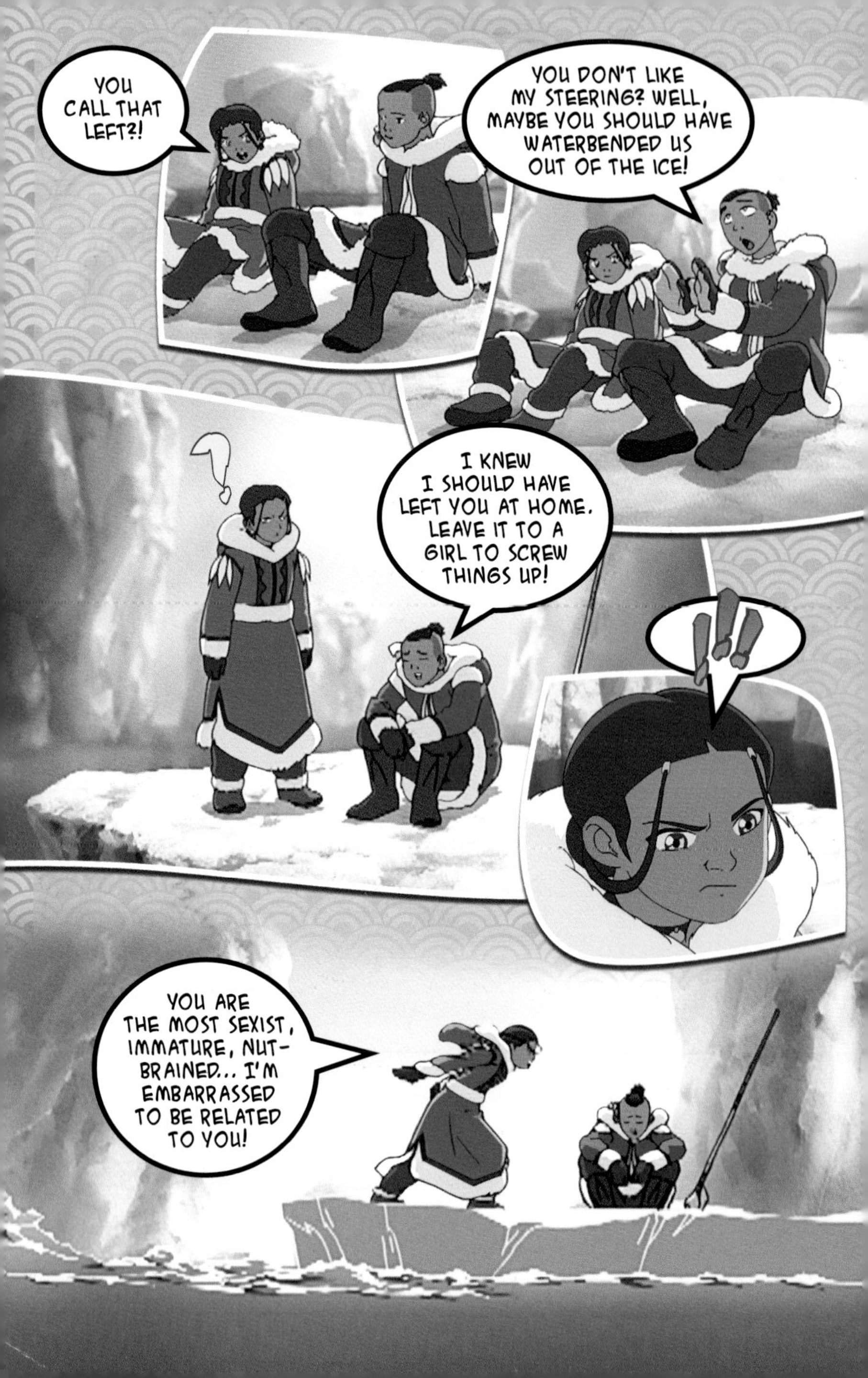
YOU CALL THAT LEFT?!
YOU DON'T LIKE MY STEERING? WELL, MAYBE YOU SHOULD HAVE WATERBENDED US OUT OF THE ICE!
I KNEW I SHOULD HAVE LEFT YOU AT HOME. LEAVE IT TO A GIRL TO SCREW THINGS UP!
YOU ARE THE MOST SEXIST, IMMATURE, NUT-BRAINED... I'M EMBARRASSED TO BE RELATED TO YOU!

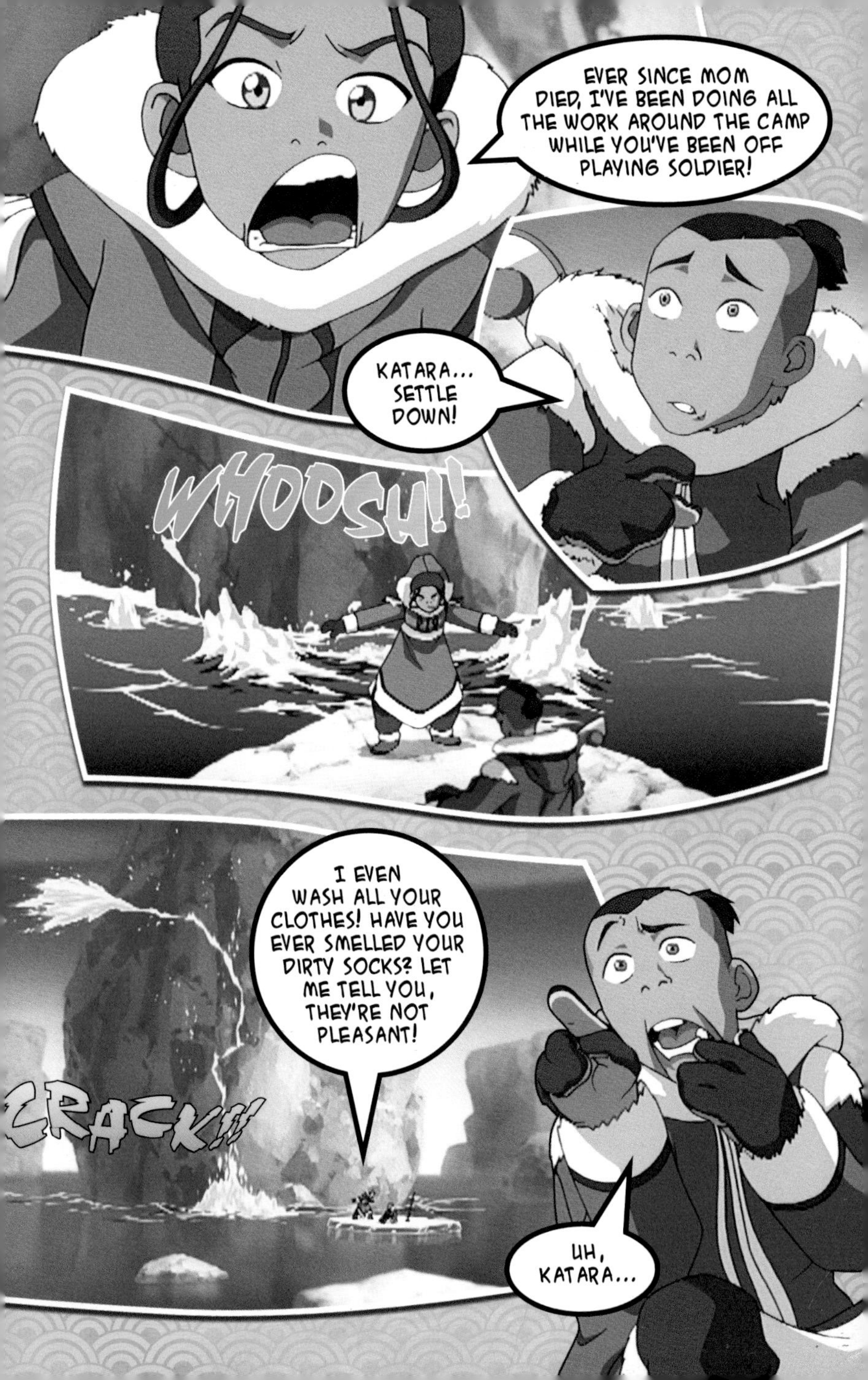
EVER SINCE MOM DIED, I'VE BEEN DOING ALL THE WORK AROUND THE CAMP WHILE YOU'VE BEEN OFF PLAYING SOLDIER!
KATARA... SETTLE DOWN!
WHOOSH!!
I EVEN WASH ALL YOUR CLOTHES! HAVE YOU EVER SMELLED YOUR DIRTY SOCKS? LET ME TELL YOU, THEY'RE NOT PLEASANT!
CRACK!!
UH, KATARA...

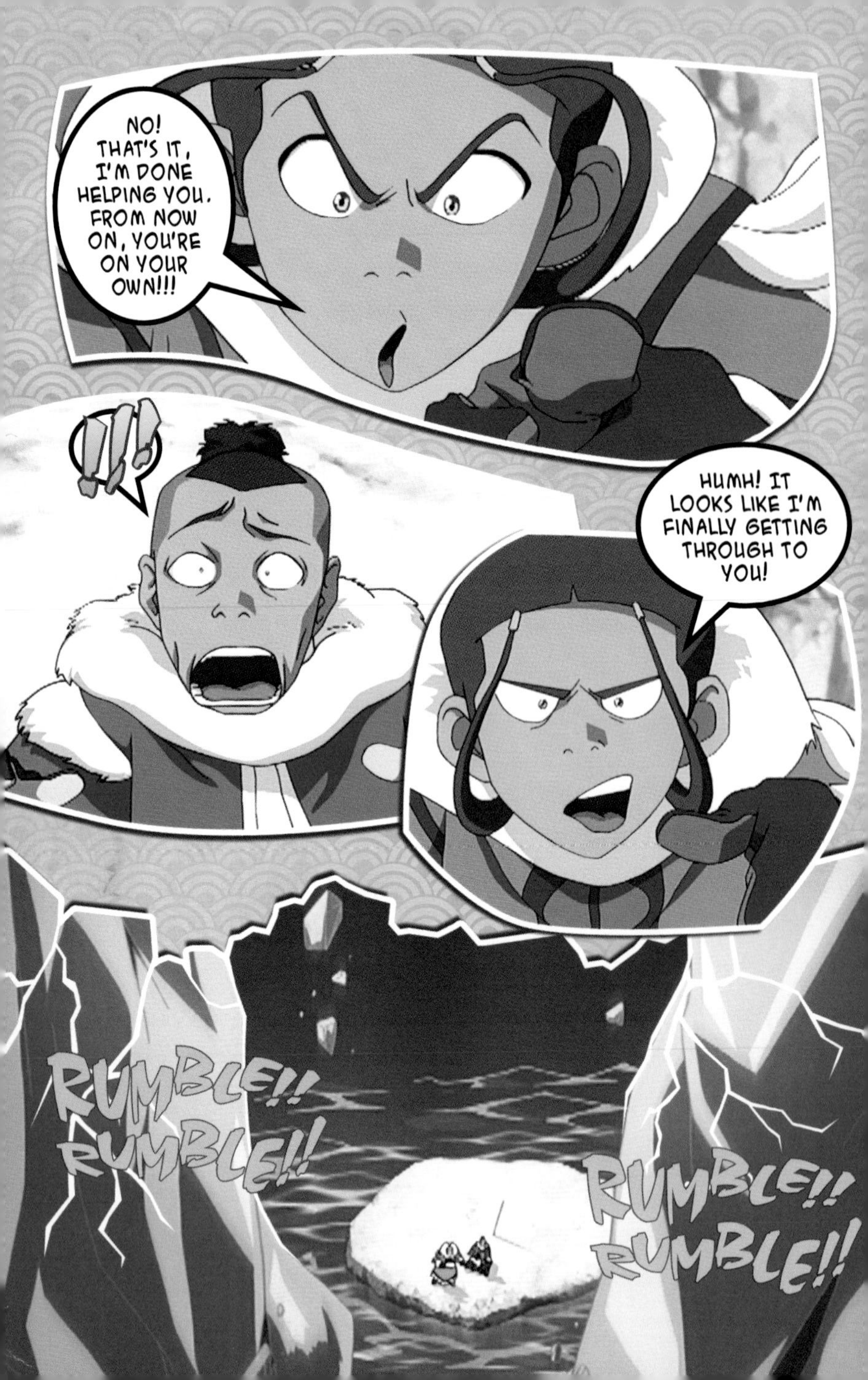
NO! THAT'S IT, I'M DONE HELPING YOU. FROM NOW ON, YOU'RE ON YOUR OWN!!!
!!
HUMH! IT LOOKS LIKE I'M FINALLY GETTING THROUGH TO YOU!
RUMBLE!! RUMBLE!!
RUMBLE!! RUMBLE!!

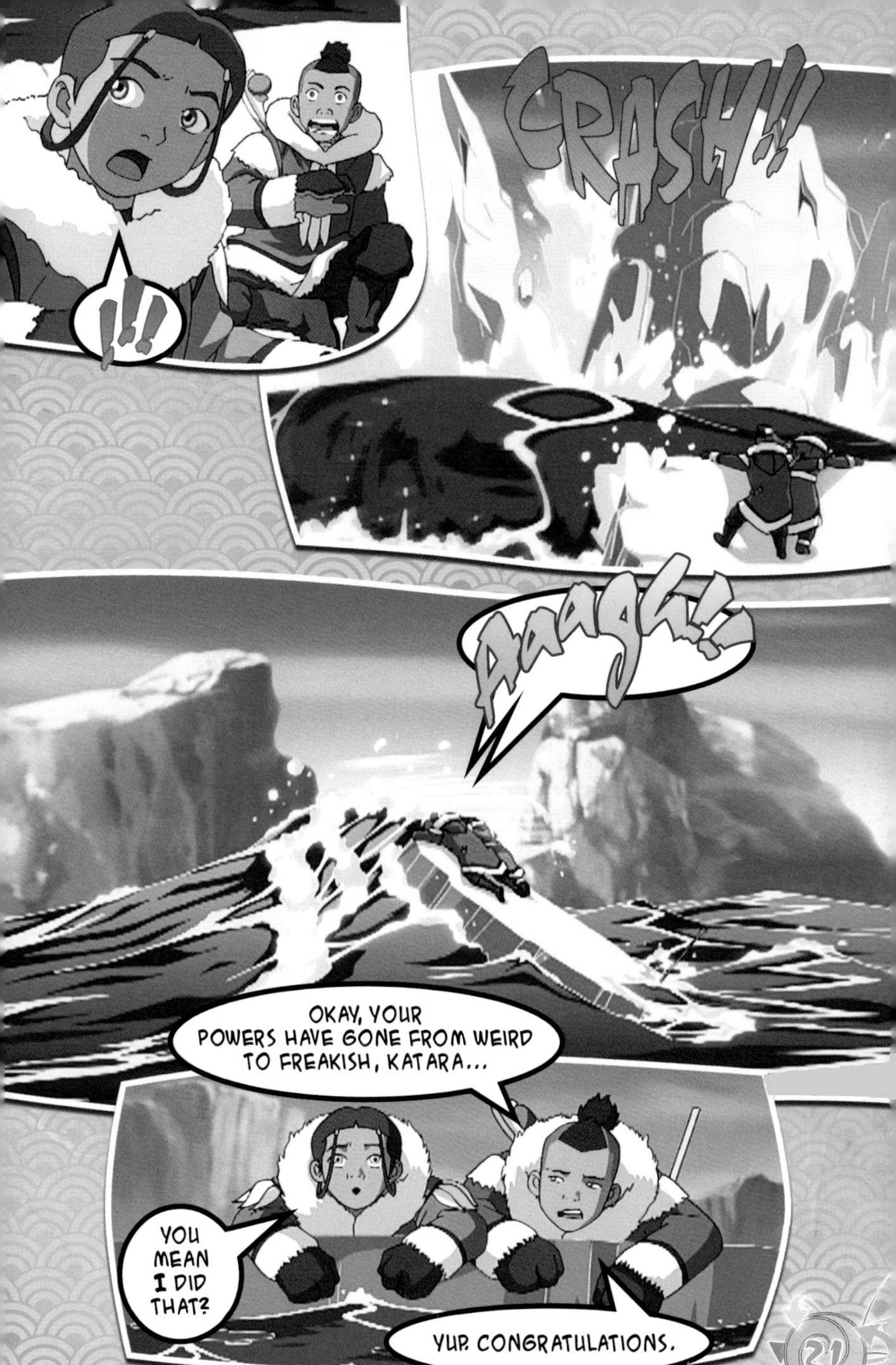
!!
CRASH!!
Aaagh!!
OKAY, YOUR POWERS HAVE GONE FROM WEIRD TO FREAKISH, KATARA...
YOU MEAN I DID THAT?
YUP. CONGRATULATIONS.

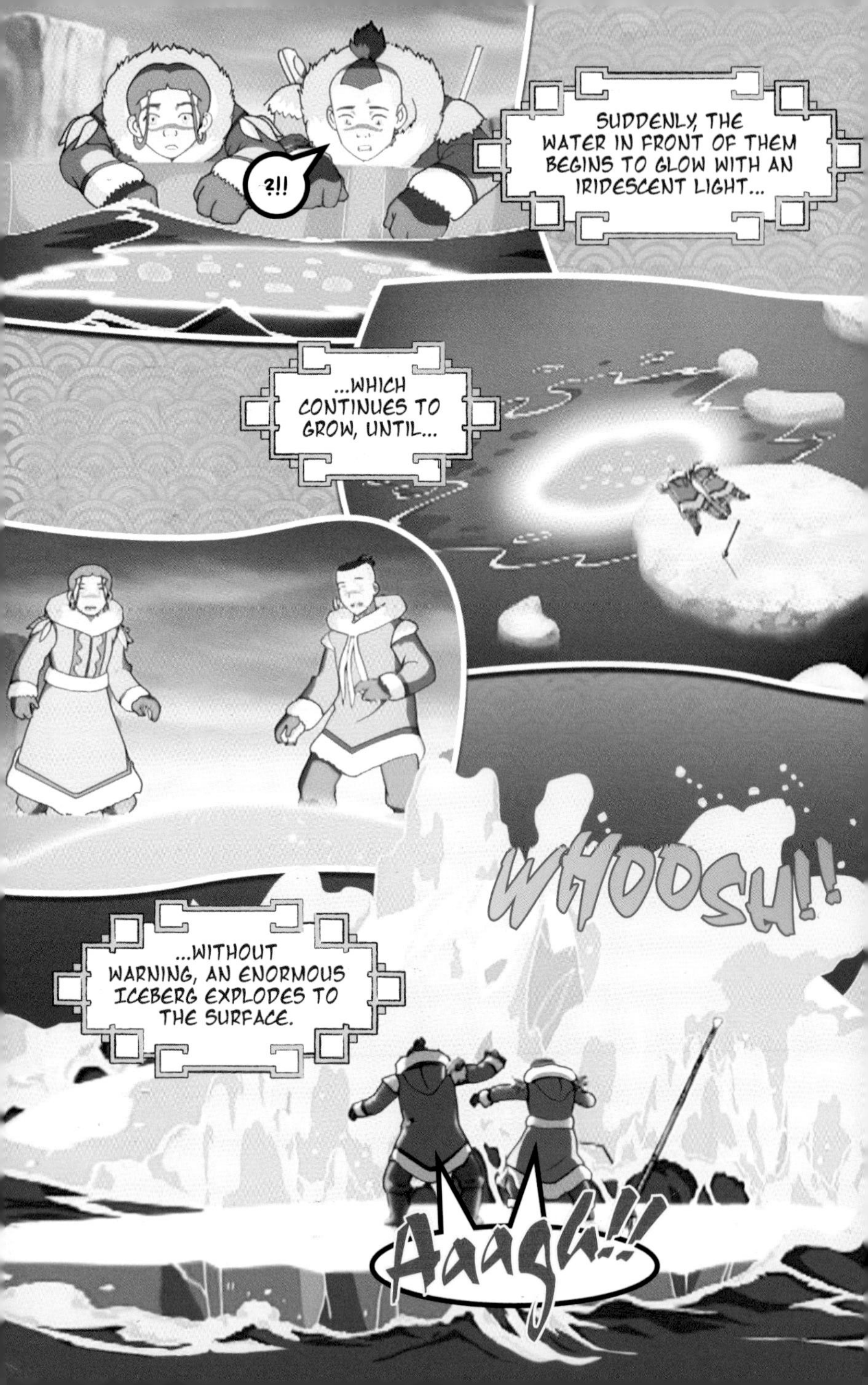
?!!
SUDDENLY, THE WATER IN FRONT OF THEM BEGINS TO GLOW WITH AN IRIDESCENT LIGHT...
...WHICH CONTINUES TO GROW, UNTIL...
...WITHOUT WARNING, AN ENORMOUS ICEBERG EXPLODES TO THE SURFACE.
WHOOSH!!
Aaagh!!

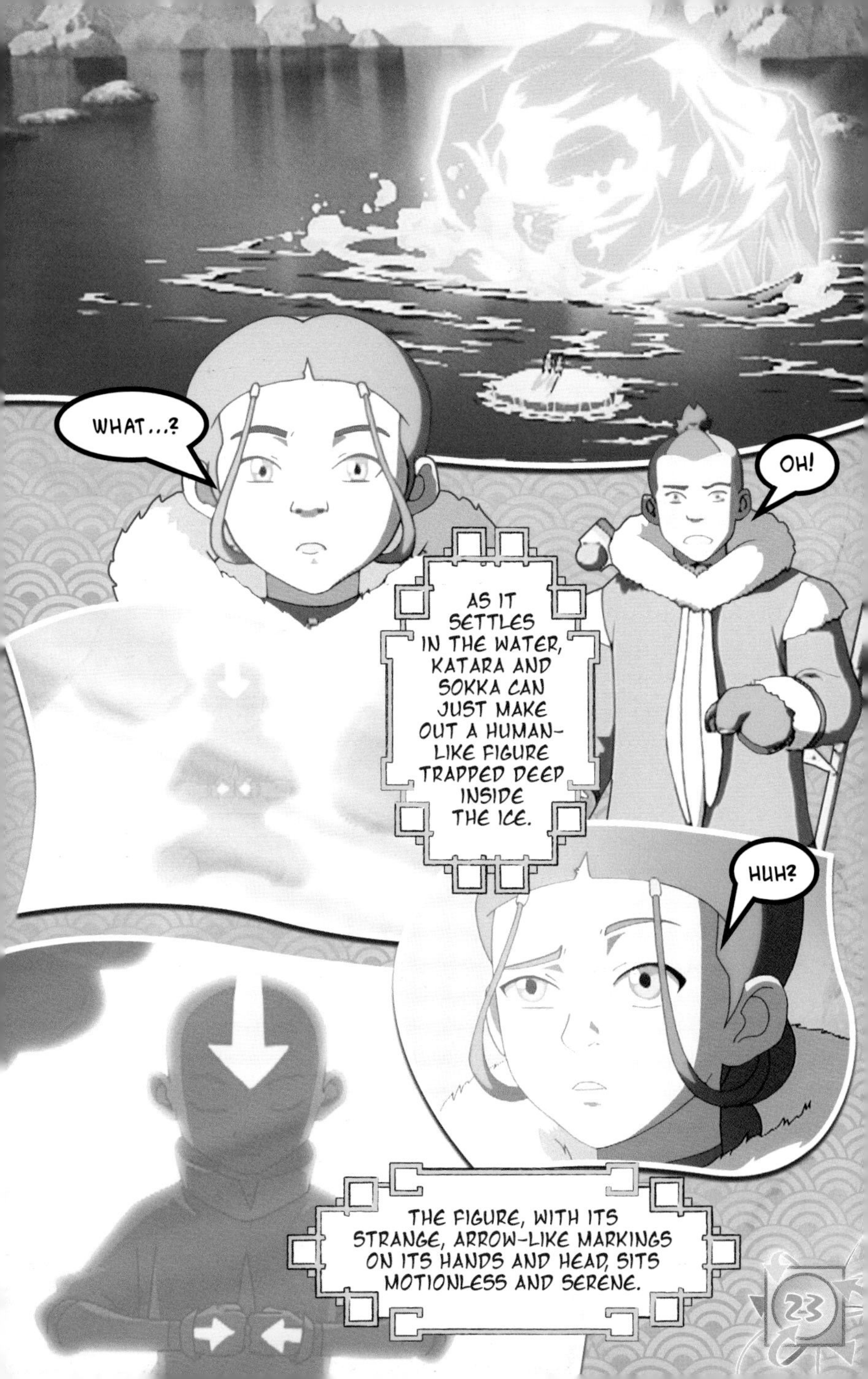
WHAT...?
OH!
AS IT SETTLES IN THE WATER, KATARA AND SOKKA CAN JUST MAKE OUT A HUMAN-LIKE FIGURE TRAPPED DEEP INSIDE THE ICE.
HUH?
THE FIGURE, WITH ITS STRANGE, ARROW-LIKE MARKINGS ON ITS HANDS AND HEAD, SITS MOTIONLESS AND SERENE.

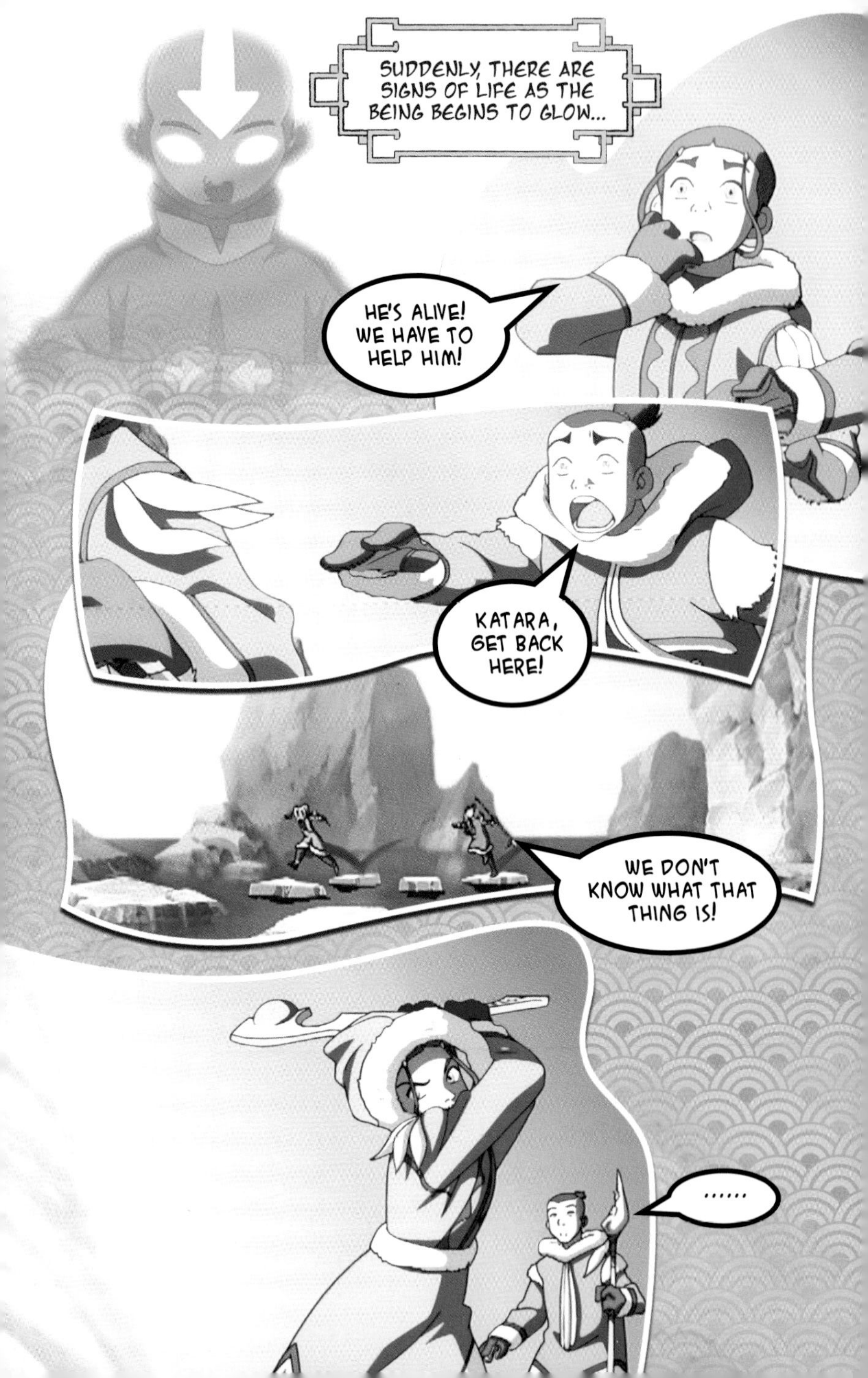
SUDDENLY, THERE ARE SIGNS OF LIFE AS THE BEING BEGINS TO GLOW...
HE'S ALIVE! WE HAVE TO HELP HIM!
KATARA, GET BACK HERE!
WE DON'T KNOW WHAT THAT THING IS!
......

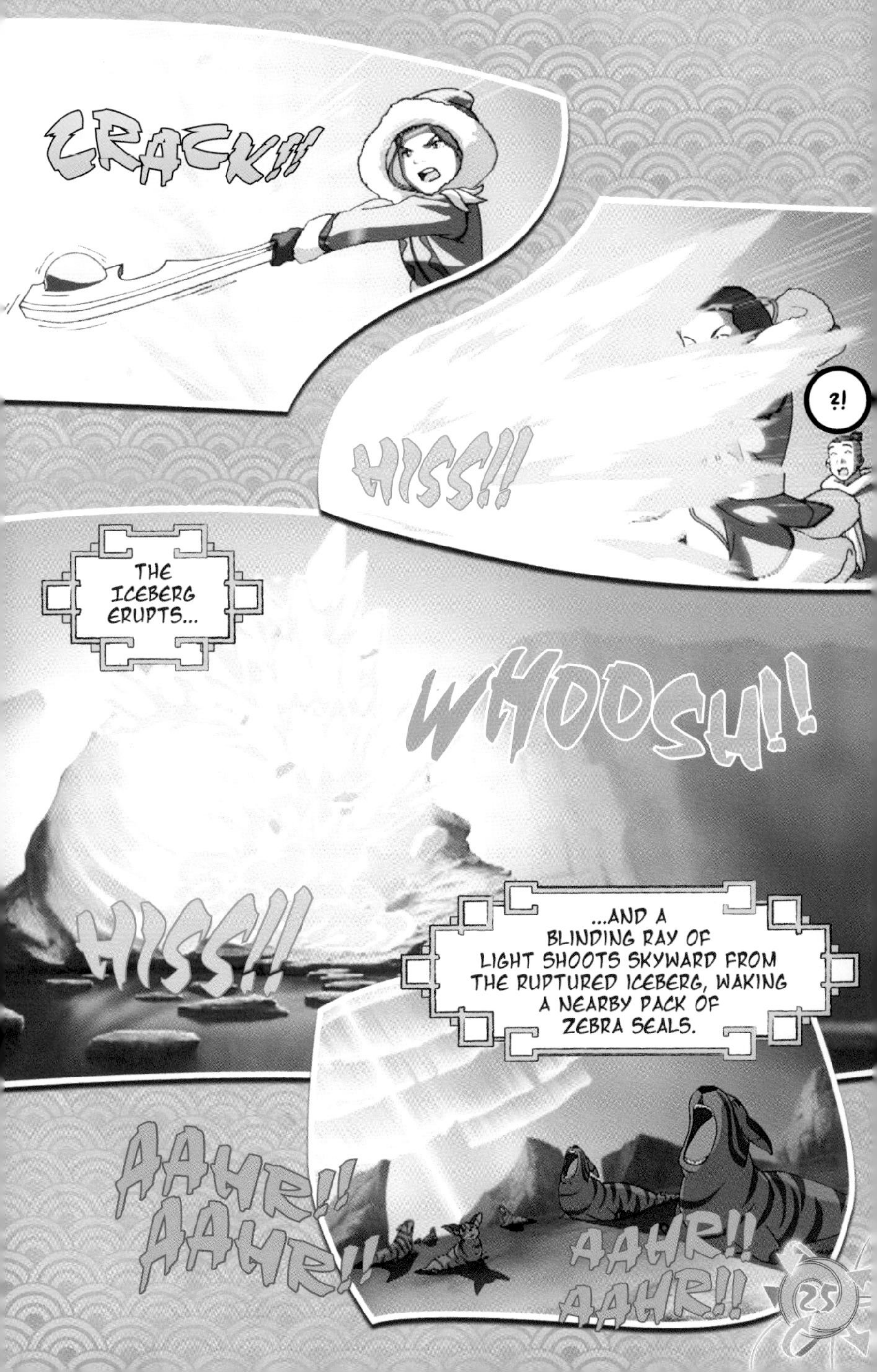
CRACK!!
HISS!!
?!
THE ICEBERG ERUPTS...
WHOOSH!!
HISS!!
...AND A BLINDING RAY OF LIGHT SHOOTS SKYWARD FROM THE RUPTURED ICEBERG, WAKING A NEARBY PACK OF ZEBRA SEALS.
AAHR!! AAHR!!
AAHR!! AAHR!!

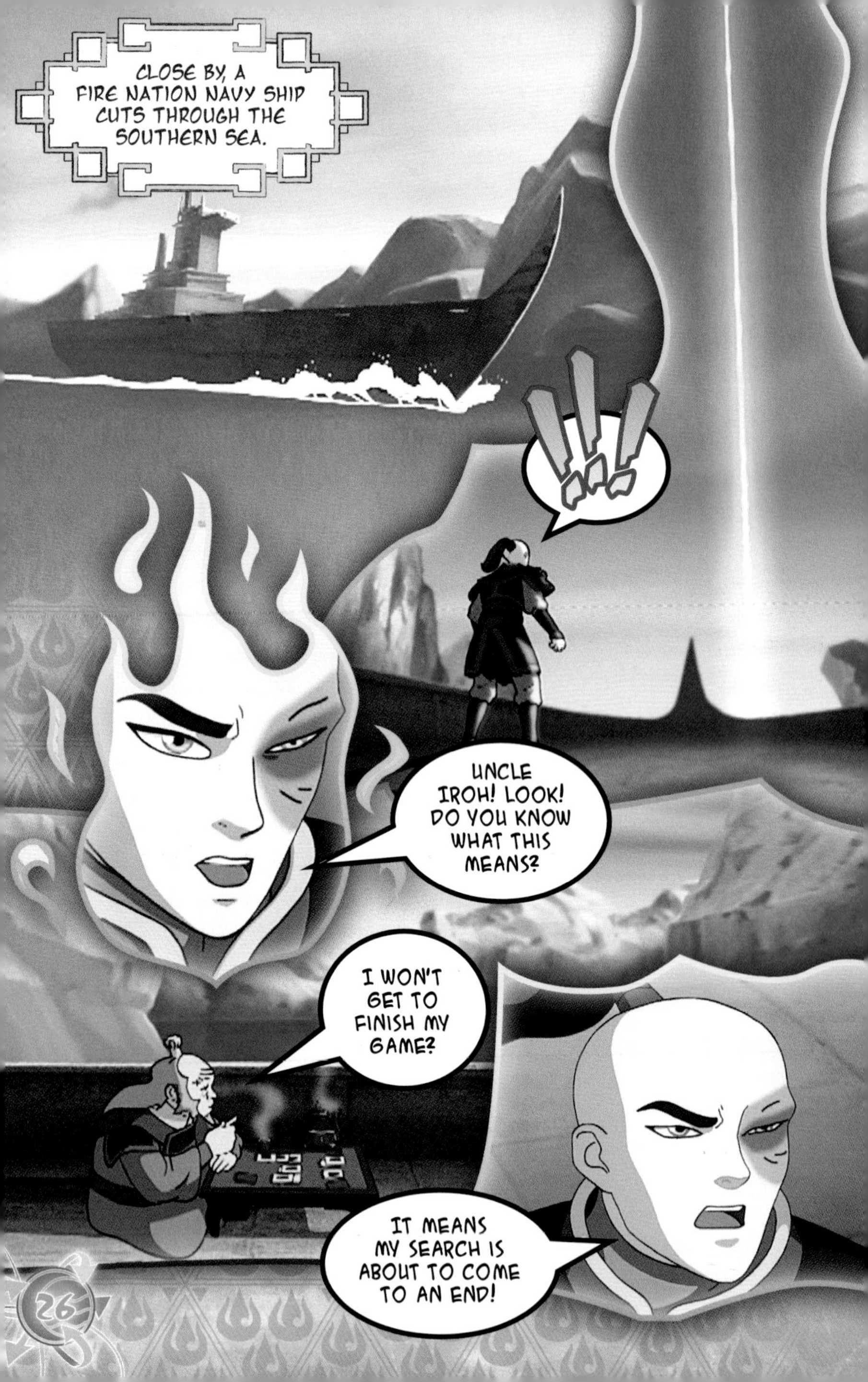

CLOSE BY, A FIRE NATION NAVY SHIP CUTS THROUGH THE SOUTHERN SEA.
!!!
UNCLE IROH! LOOK! DO YOU KNOW WHAT THIS MEANS?
I WON'T GET TO FINISH MY GAME?
IT MEANS MY SEARCH IS ABOUT TO COME TO AN END!

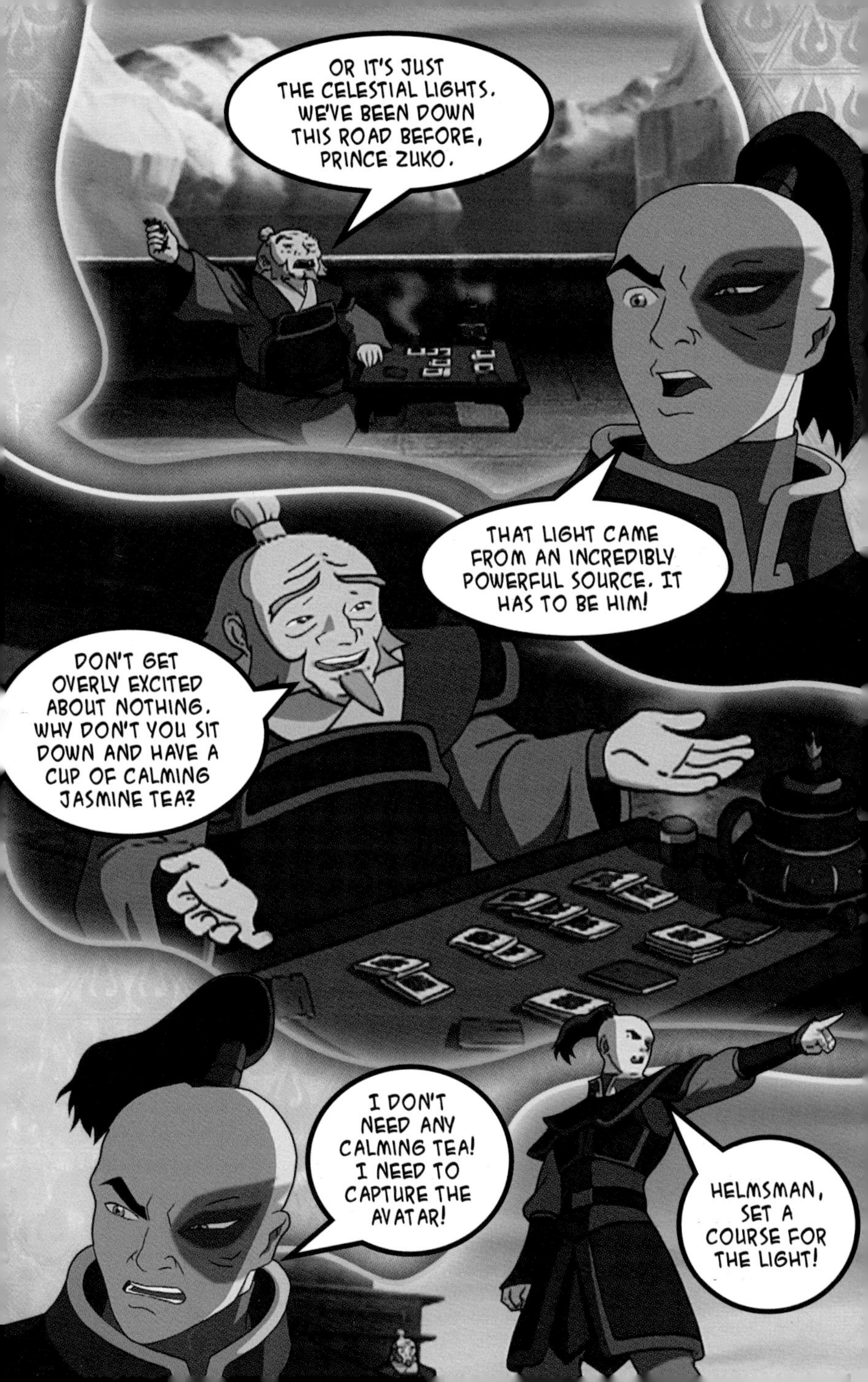
OR IT'S JUST THE CELESTIAL LIGHTS. WE'VE BEEN DOWN THIS ROAD BEFORE, PRINCE ZUKO.
THAT LIGHT CAME FROM AN INCREDIBLY POWERFUL SOURCE. IT HAS TO BE HIM!
DON'T GET OVERLY EXCITED ABOUT NOTHING. WHY DON'T YOU SIT DOWN AND HAVE A CUP OF CALMING JASMINE TEA?
I DON'T NEED ANY CALMING TEA! I NEED TO CAPTURE THE AVATAR!
HELMSMAN, SET A COURSE FOR THE LIGHT!

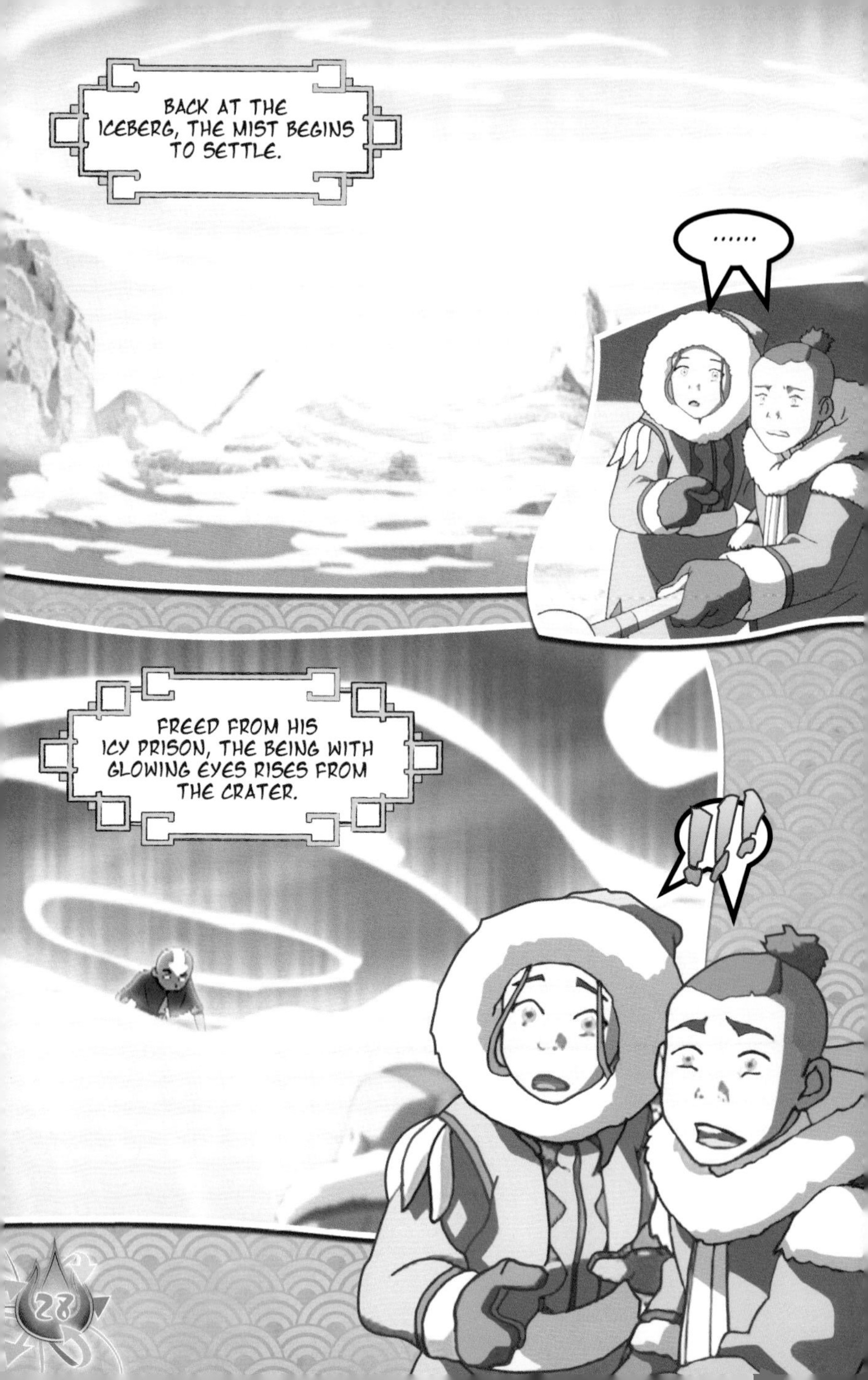
BACK AT THE ICEBERG, THE MIST BEGINS TO SETTLE.
......
FREED FROM HIS ICY PRISON, THE BEING WITH GLOWING EYES RISES FROM THE CRATER.
!!

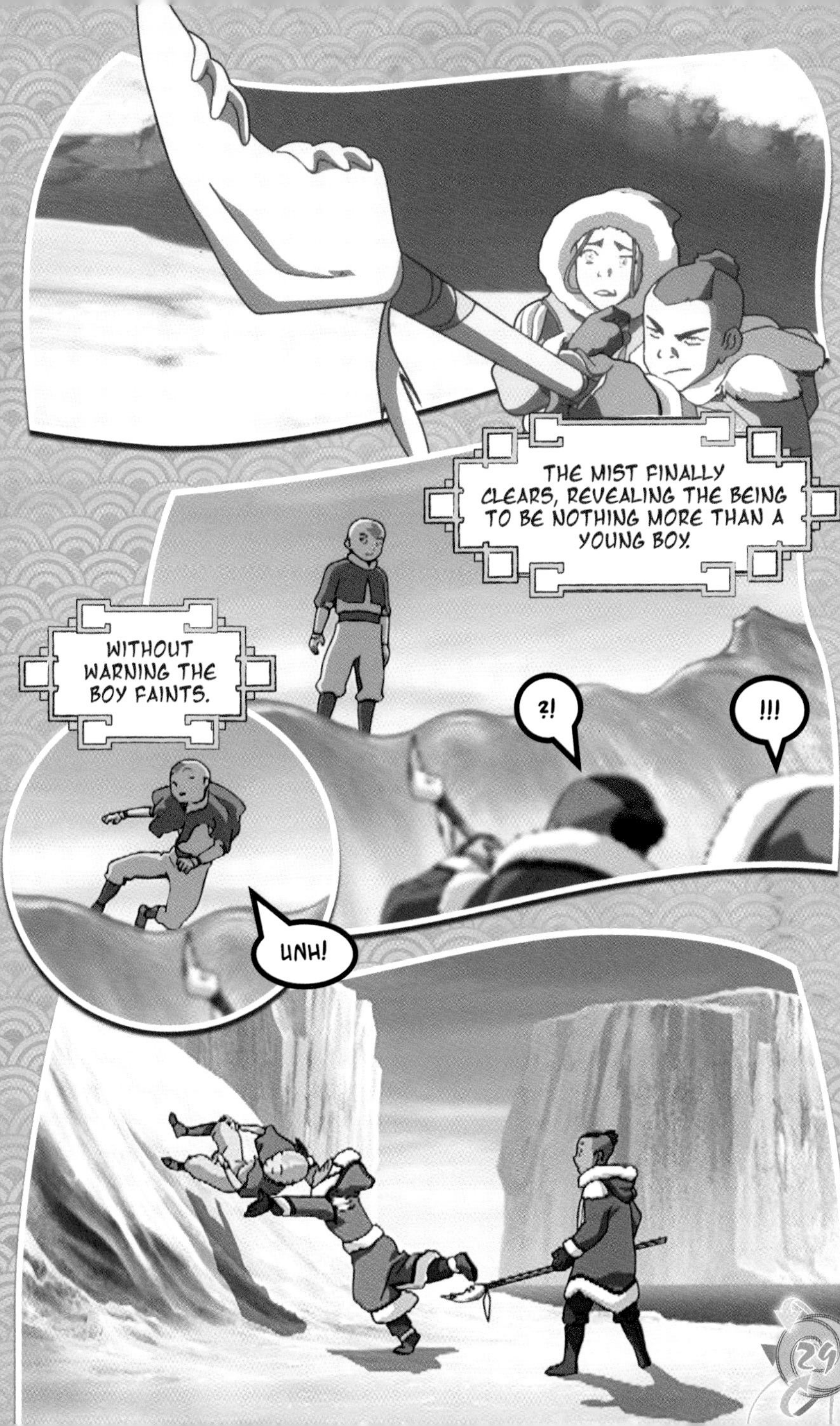
THE MIST FINALLY CLEARS, REVEALING THE BEING TO BE NOTHING MORE THAN A YOUNG BOY.
WITHOUT WARNING THE BOY FAINTS.
?!
!!!
UNH!

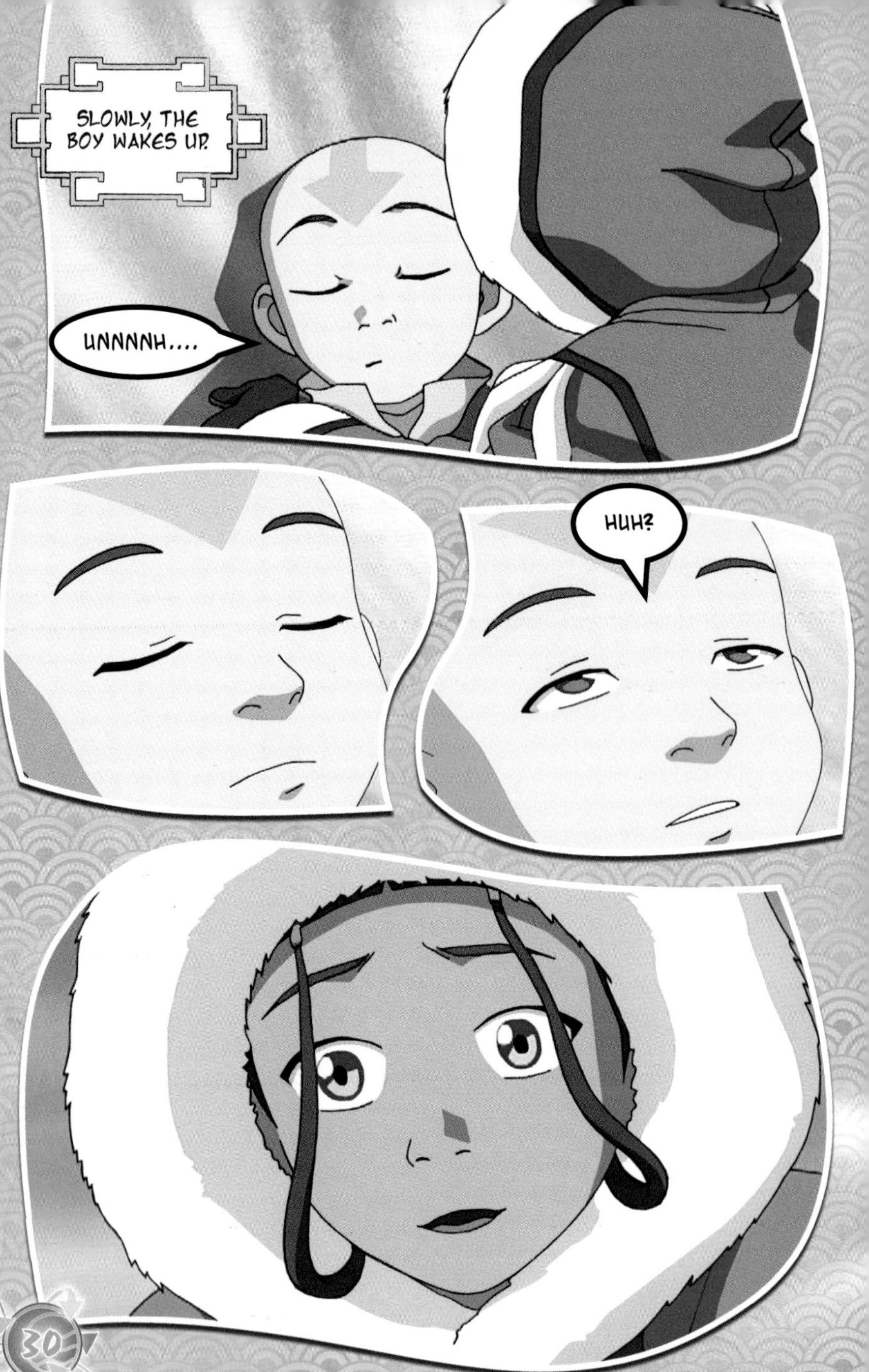
SLOWLY, THE BOY WAKES UP.
UNNNNH....
HUH?

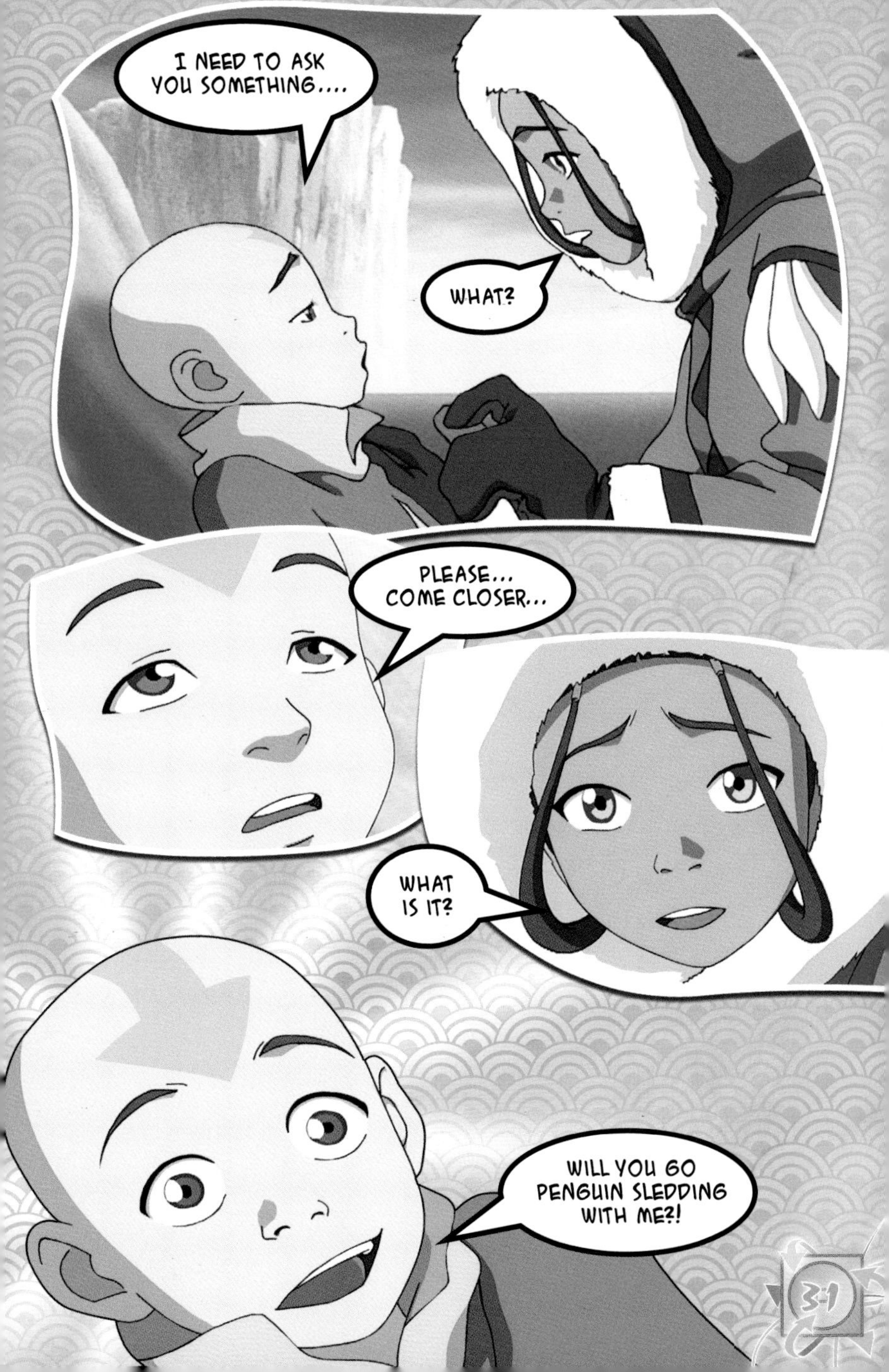
I NEED TO ASK YOU SOMETHING....
WHAT?
PLEASE... COME CLOSER...
WHAT IS IT?
WILL YOU GO PENGUIN SLEDDING WITH ME?!

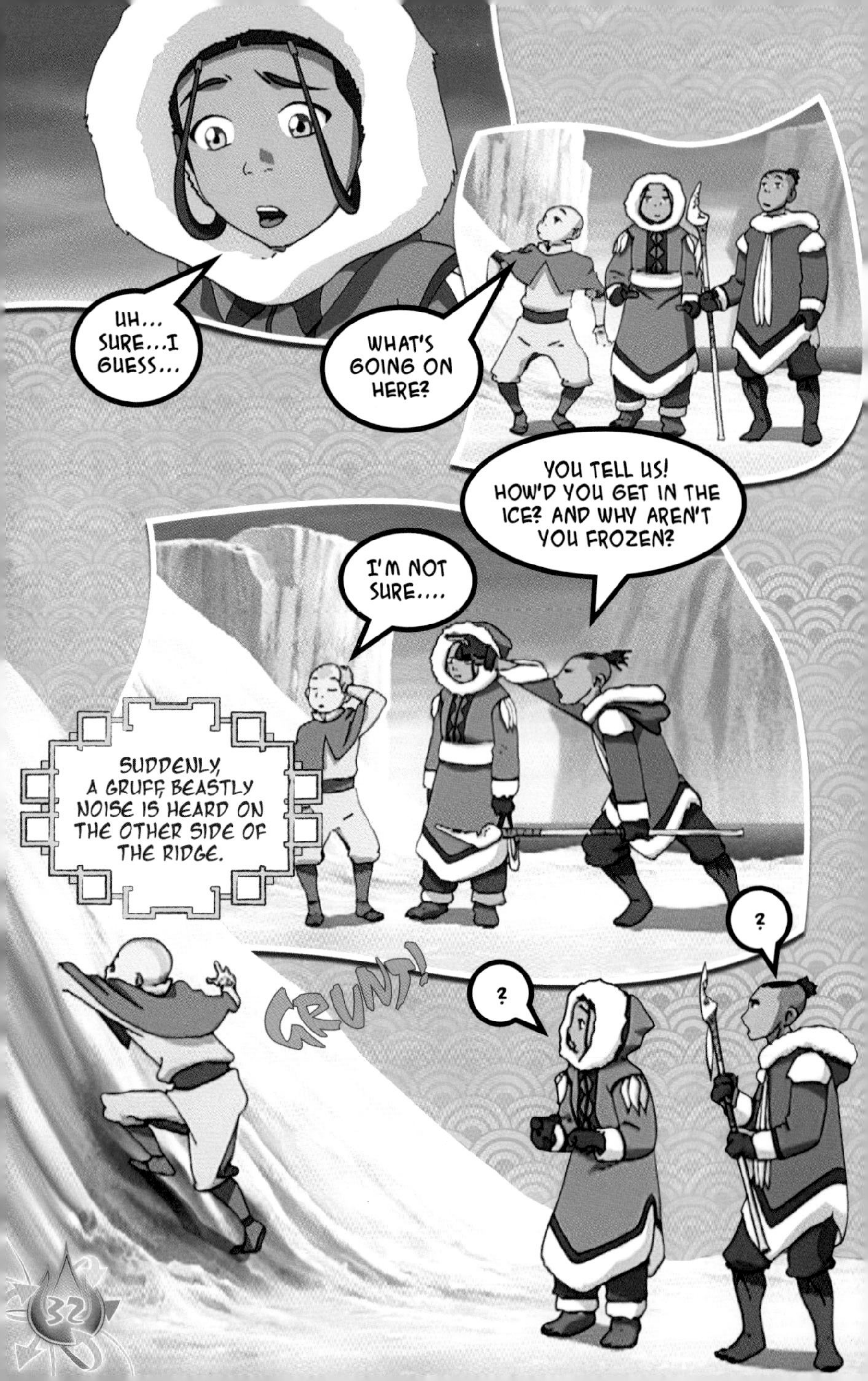

UH... SURE...I GUESS...
WHAT'S GOING ON HERE?
YOU TELL US! HOW'D YOU GET IN THE ICE? AND WHY AREN'T YOU FROZEN?
I'M NOT SURE....
SUDDENLY, A GRUFF, BEASTLY NOISE IS HEARD ON THE OTHER SIDE OF THE RIDGE.
GRUNT!
?
?

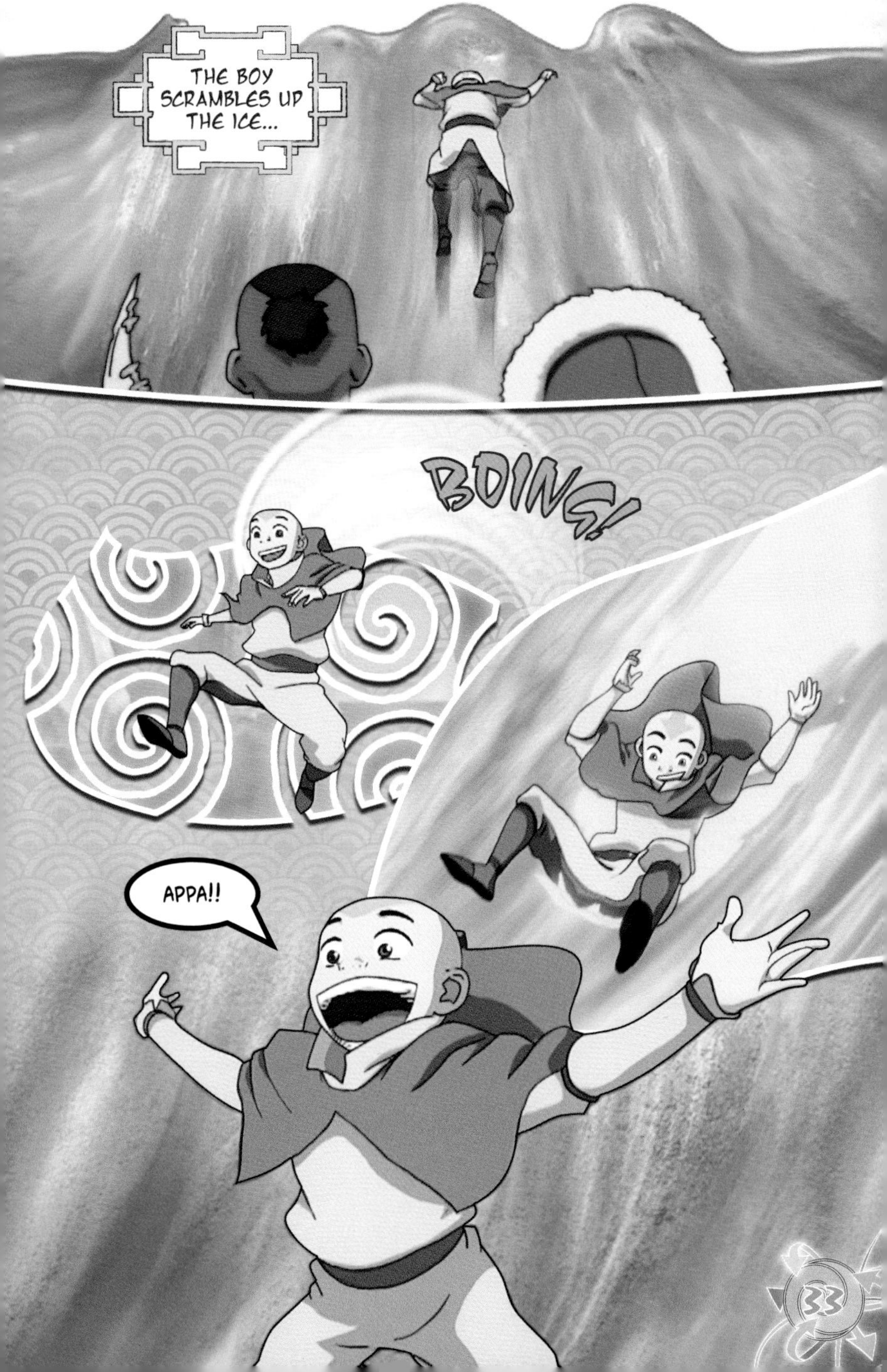
THE BOY SCRAMBLES UP THE ICE...
BOING!
APPA!!

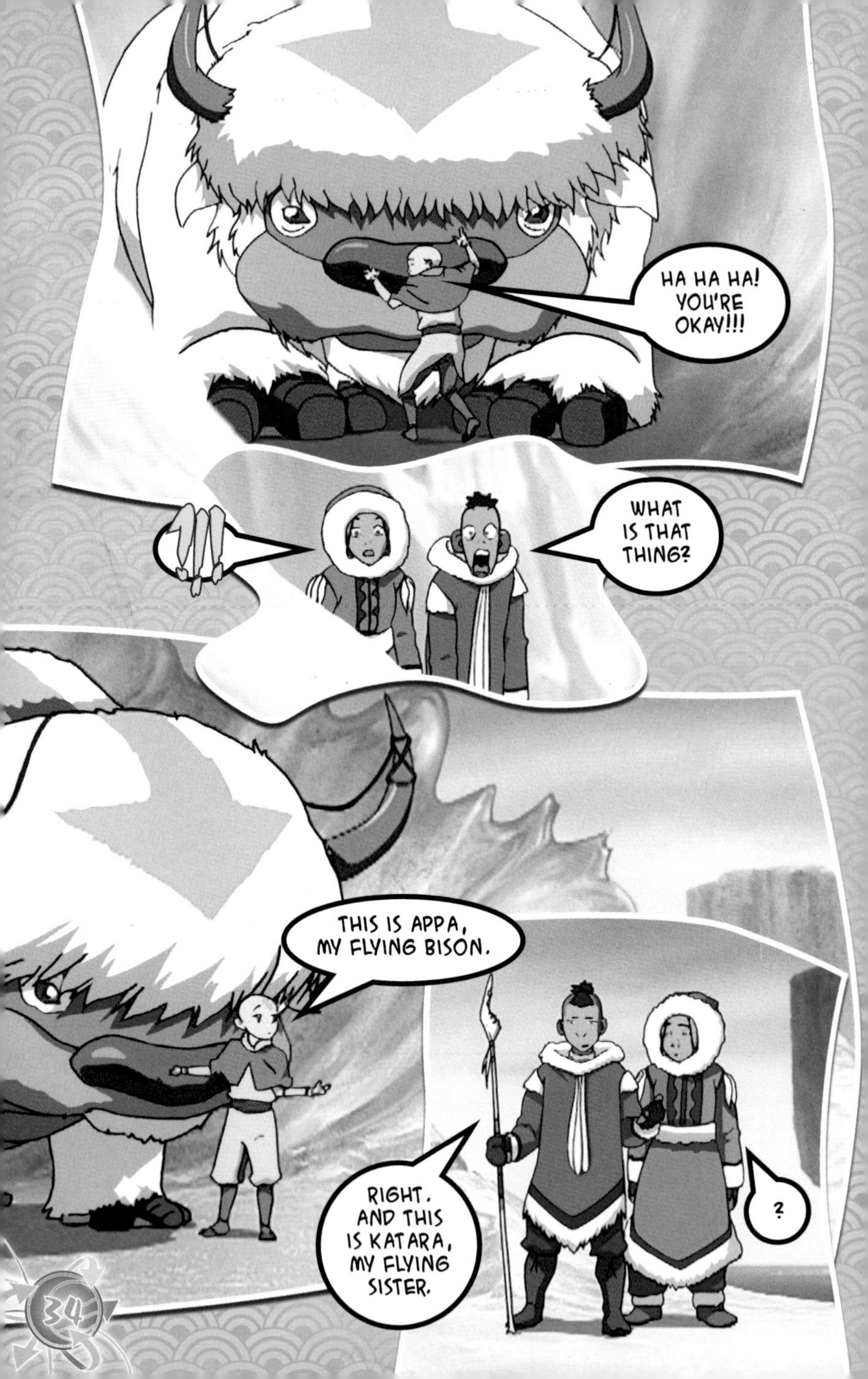
HA HA HA! YOU'RE OKAY!!!
WHAT IS THAT THING?
THIS IS APPA, MY FLYING BISON.
RIGHT. AND THIS IS KATARA, MY FLYING SISTER.
?

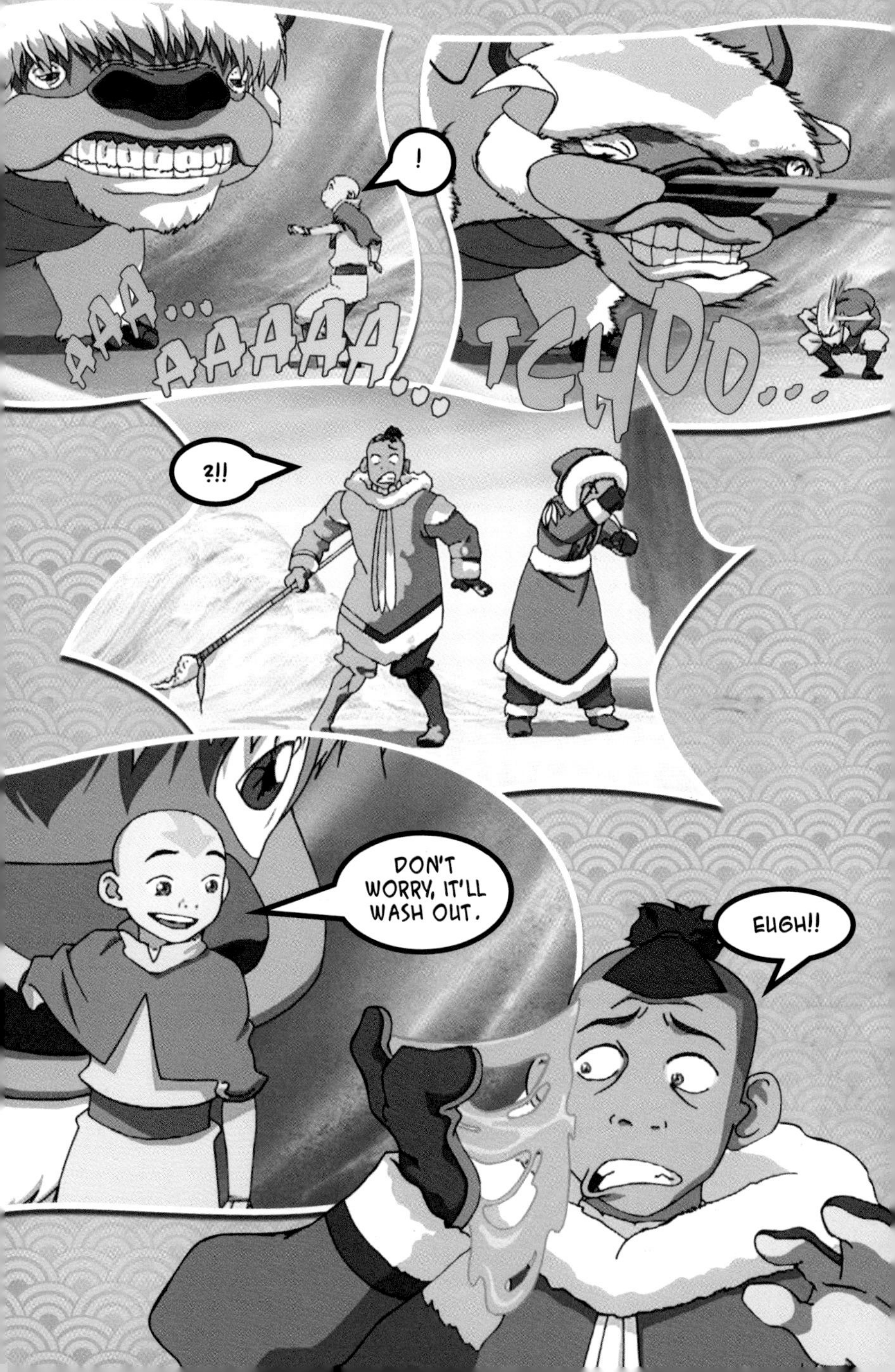
!
AAA... AAAAA...
TCHOO...
?!!
DON'T WORRY, IT'LL WASH OUT.
EUGH!!

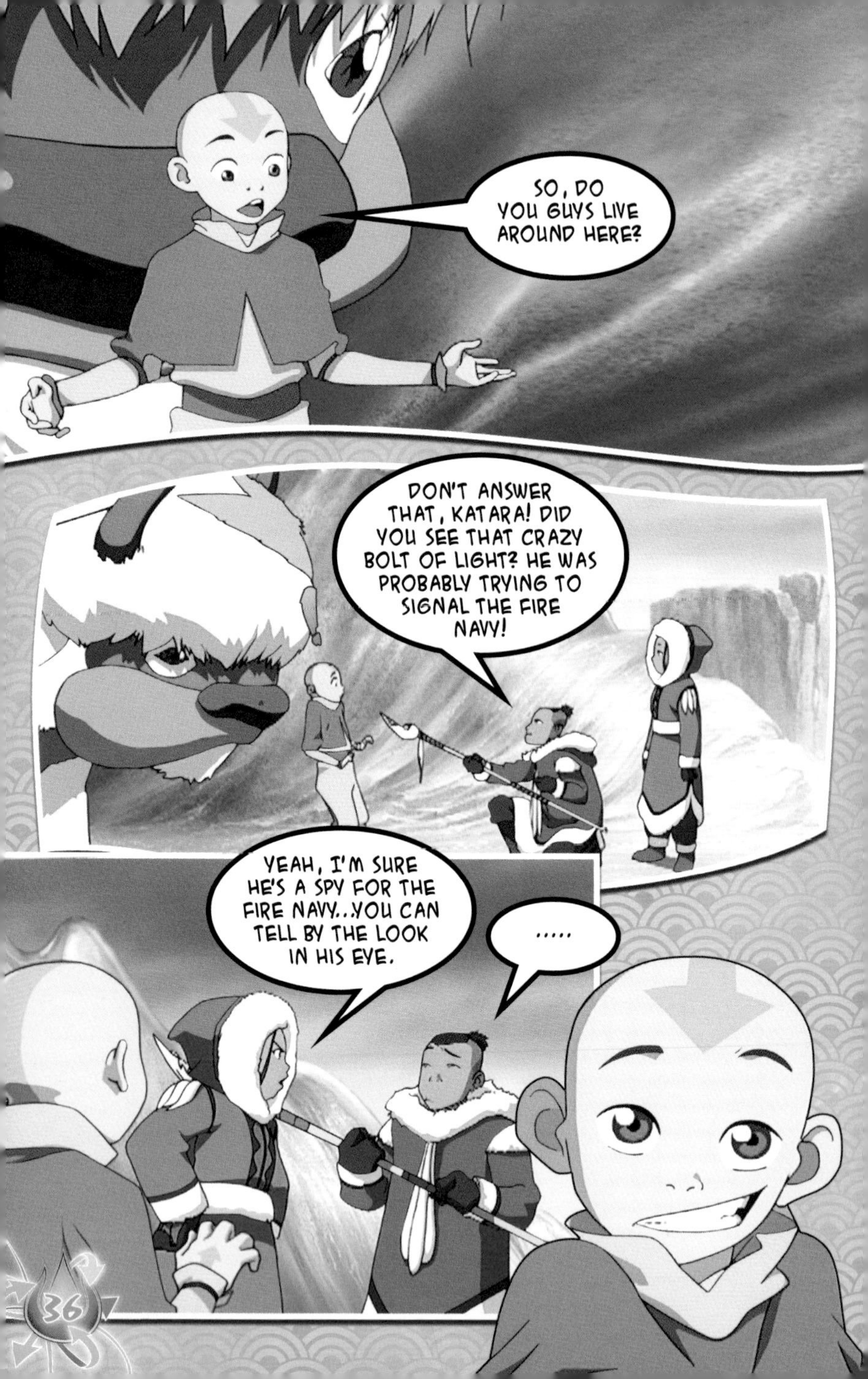
SO, DO YOU GUYS LIVE AROUND HERE?
DON'T ANSWER THAT, KATARA! DID YOU SEE THAT CRAZY BOLT OF LIGHT? HE WAS PROBABLY TRYING TO SIGNAL THE FIRE NAVY!
YEAH, I'M SURE HE'S A SPY FOR THE FIRE NAVY...YOU CAN TELL BY THE LOOK IN HIS EYE.
.....

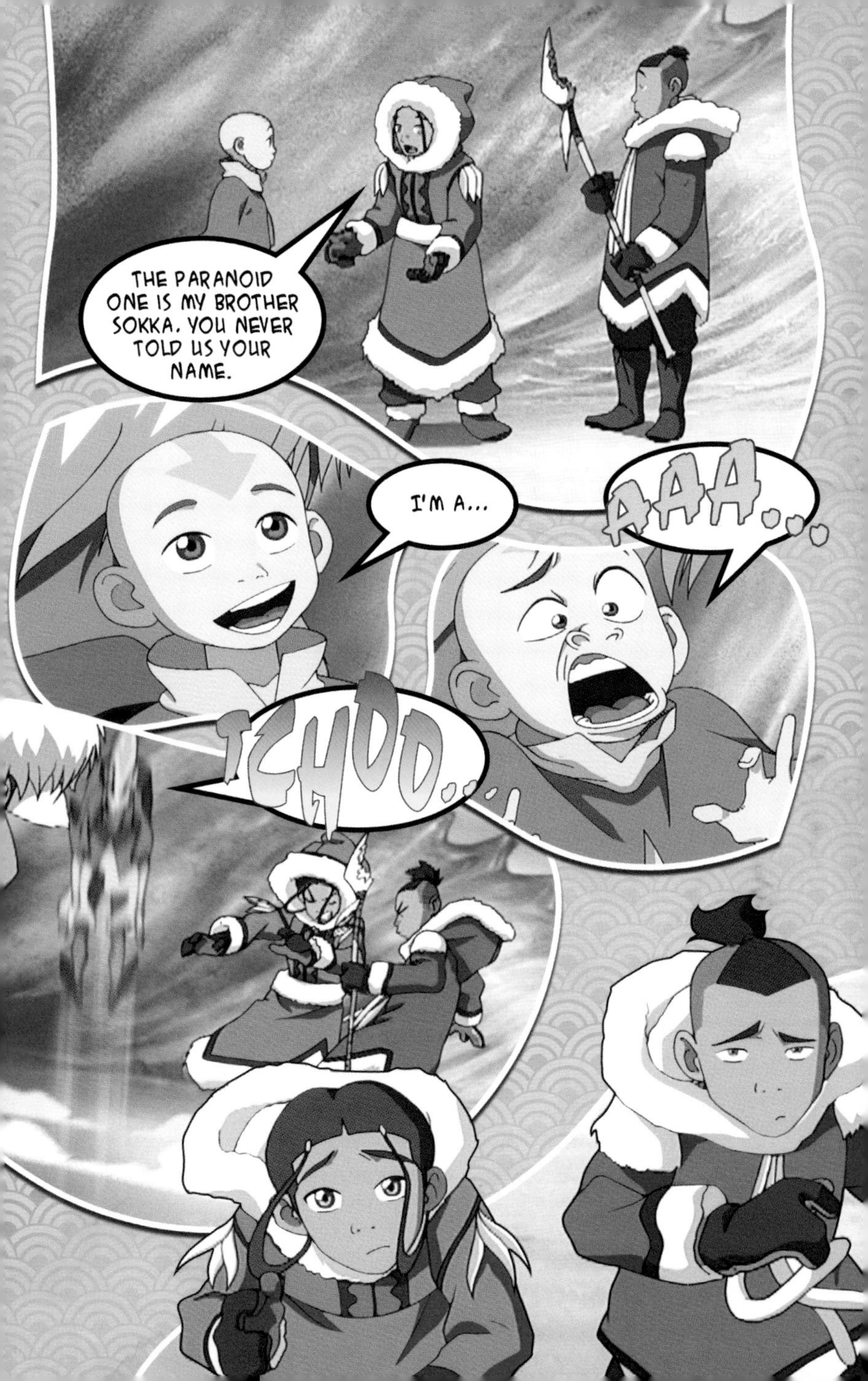
THE PARANOID ONE IS MY BROTHER SOKKA. YOU NEVER TOLD US YOUR NAME.
I'M A...
AAA...
CHOO...

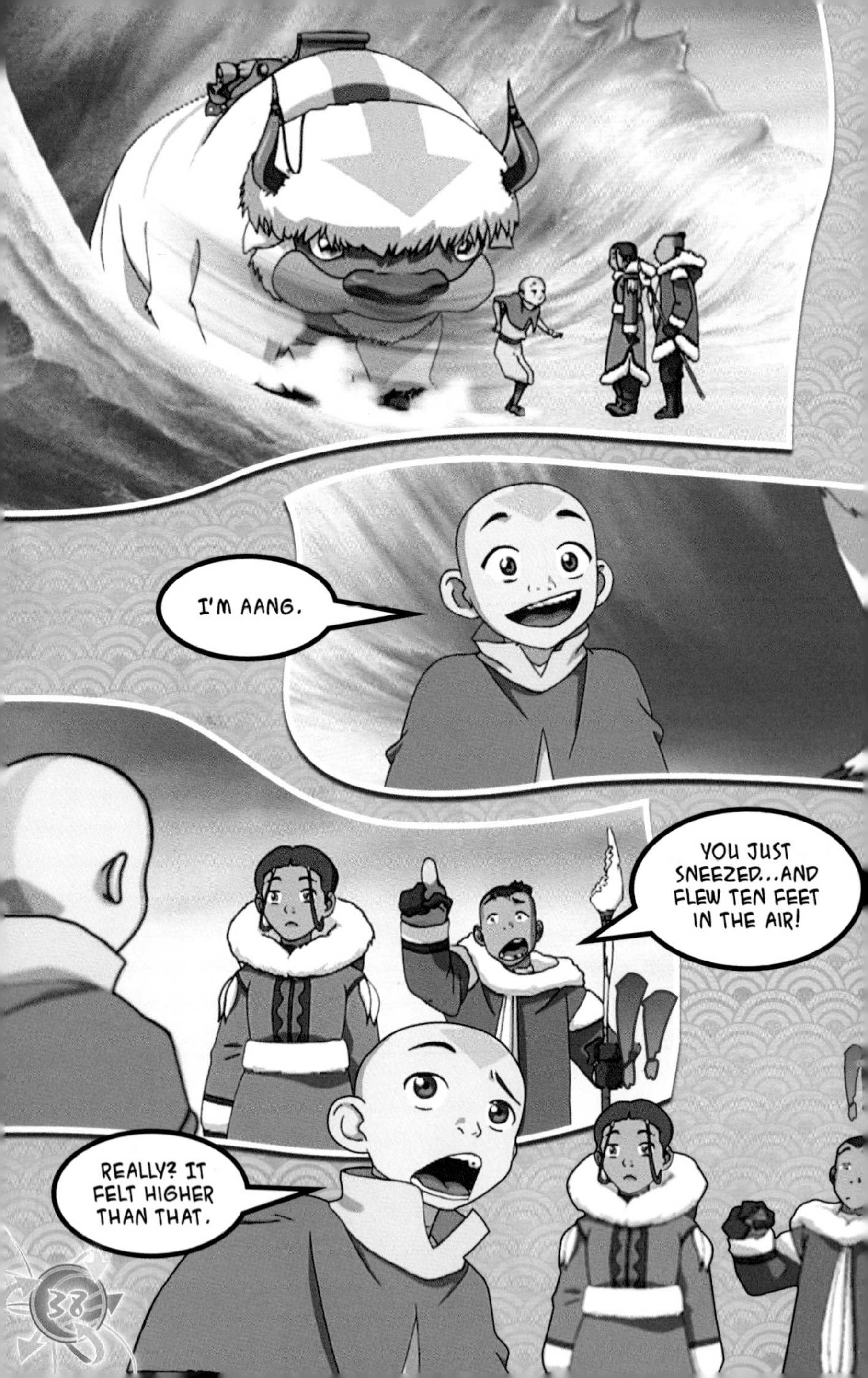
I'M AANG.
YOU JUST SNEEZED...AND FLEW TEN FEET IN THE AIR!
REALLY? IT FELT HIGHER THAN THAT.

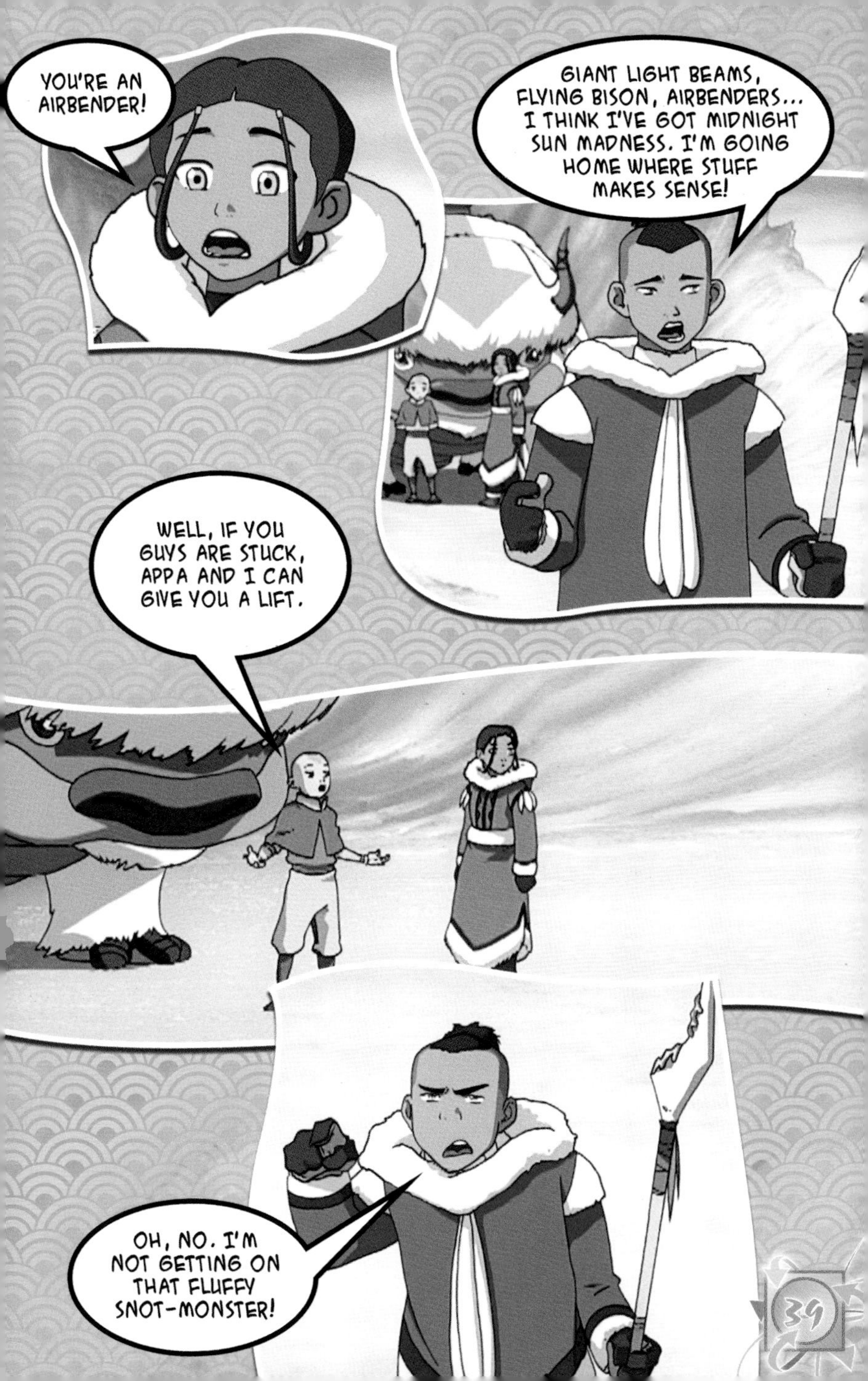
YOU'RE AN AIRBENDER!
GIANT LIGHT BEAMS, FLYING BISON, AIRBENDERS... I THINK I'VE GOT MIDNIGHT SUN MADNESS. I'M GOING HOME WHERE STUFF MAKES SENSE!
WELL, IF YOU GUYS ARE STUCK, APPA AND I CAN GIVE YOU A LIFT.
OH, NO. I'M NOT GETTING ON THAT FLUFFY SNOT-MONSTER!

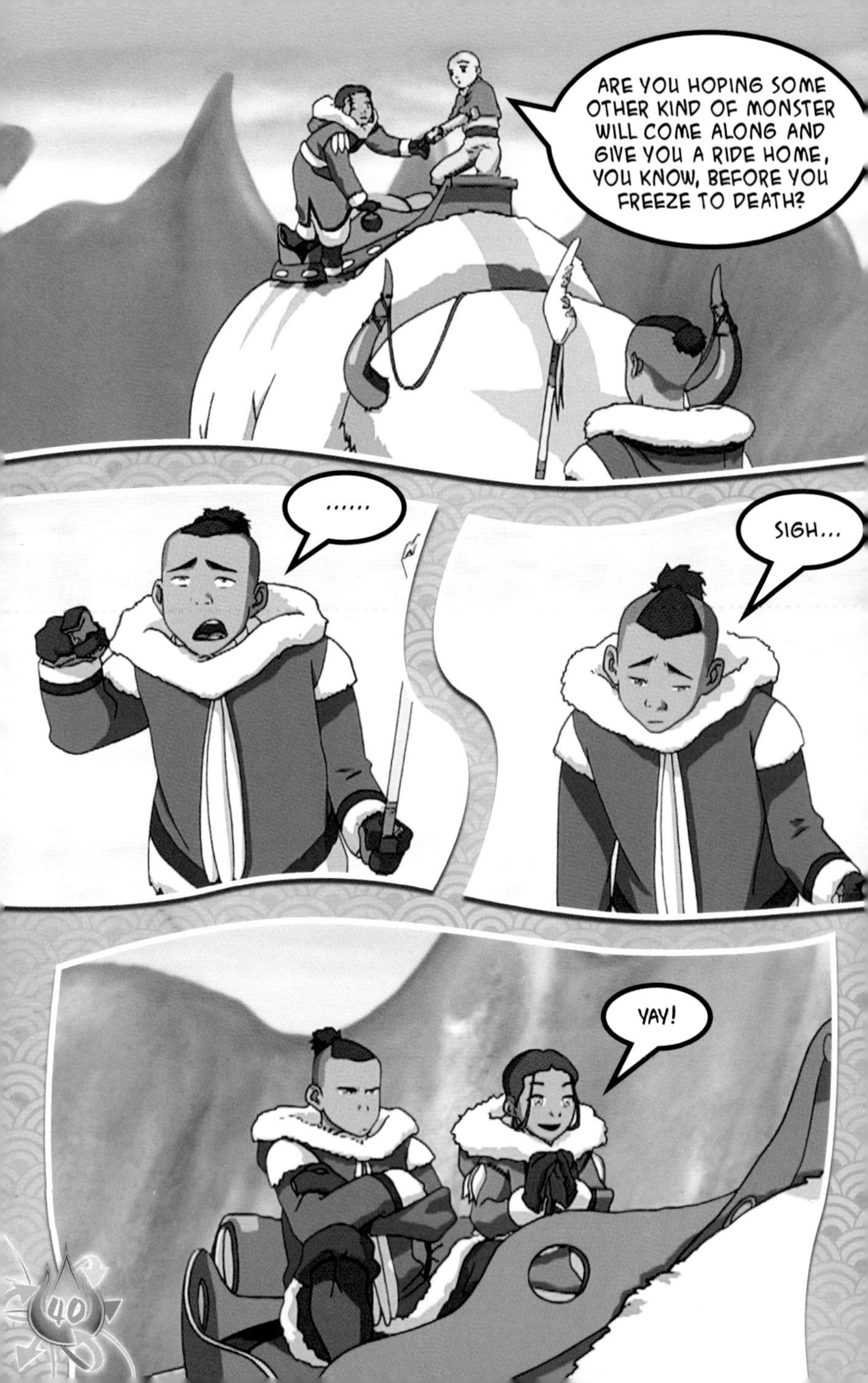
ARE YOU HOPING SOME OTHER KIND OF MONSTER WILL COME ALONG AND GIVE YOU A RIDE HOME, YOU KNOW, BEFORE YOU FREEZE TO DEATH?
......
SIGH...
YAY!

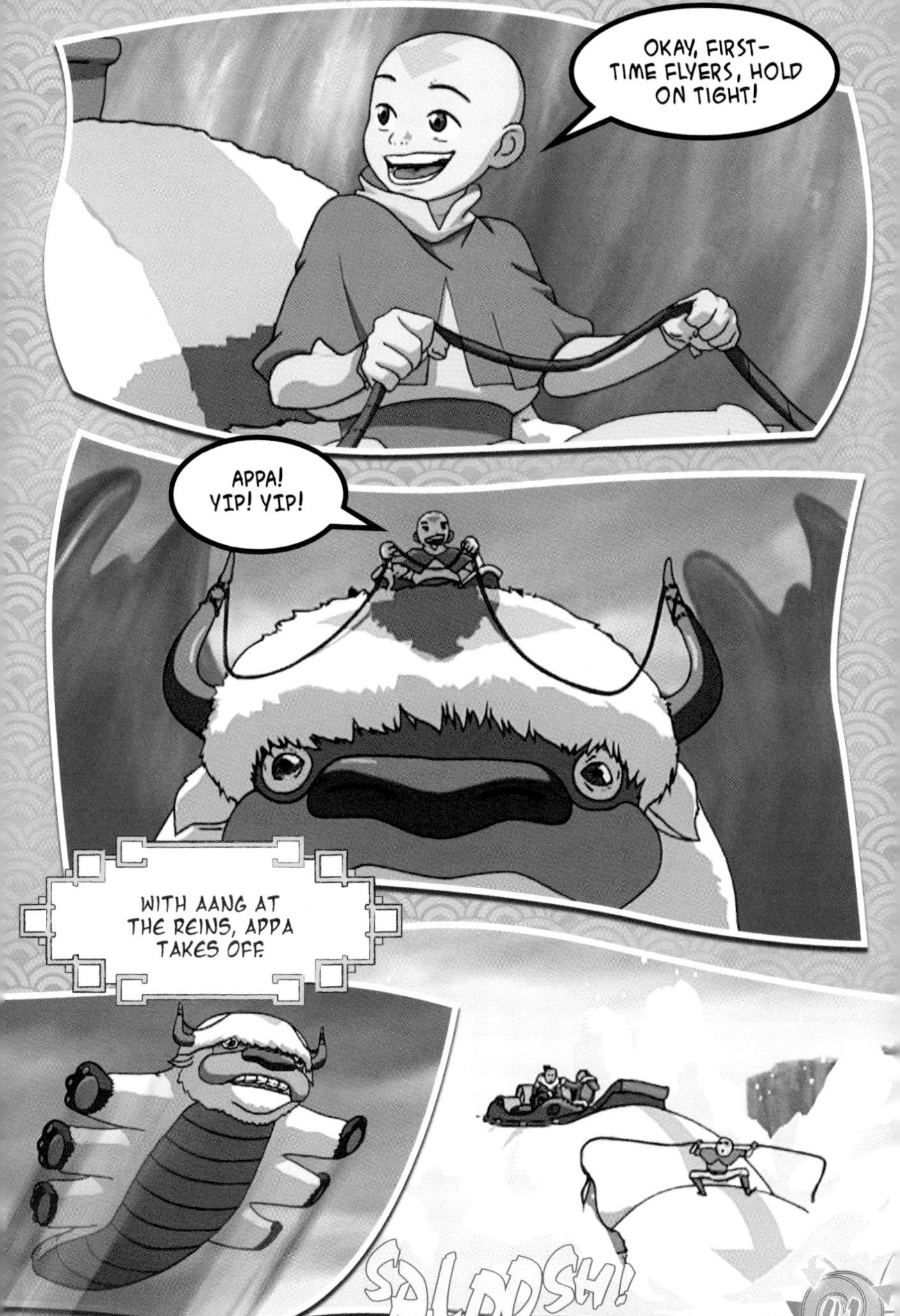
OKAY, FIRST-TIME FLYERS, HOLD ON TIGHT!
APPA! YIP! YIP!
WITH AANG AT THE REINS, APPA TAKES OFF.
SPLOOSH!

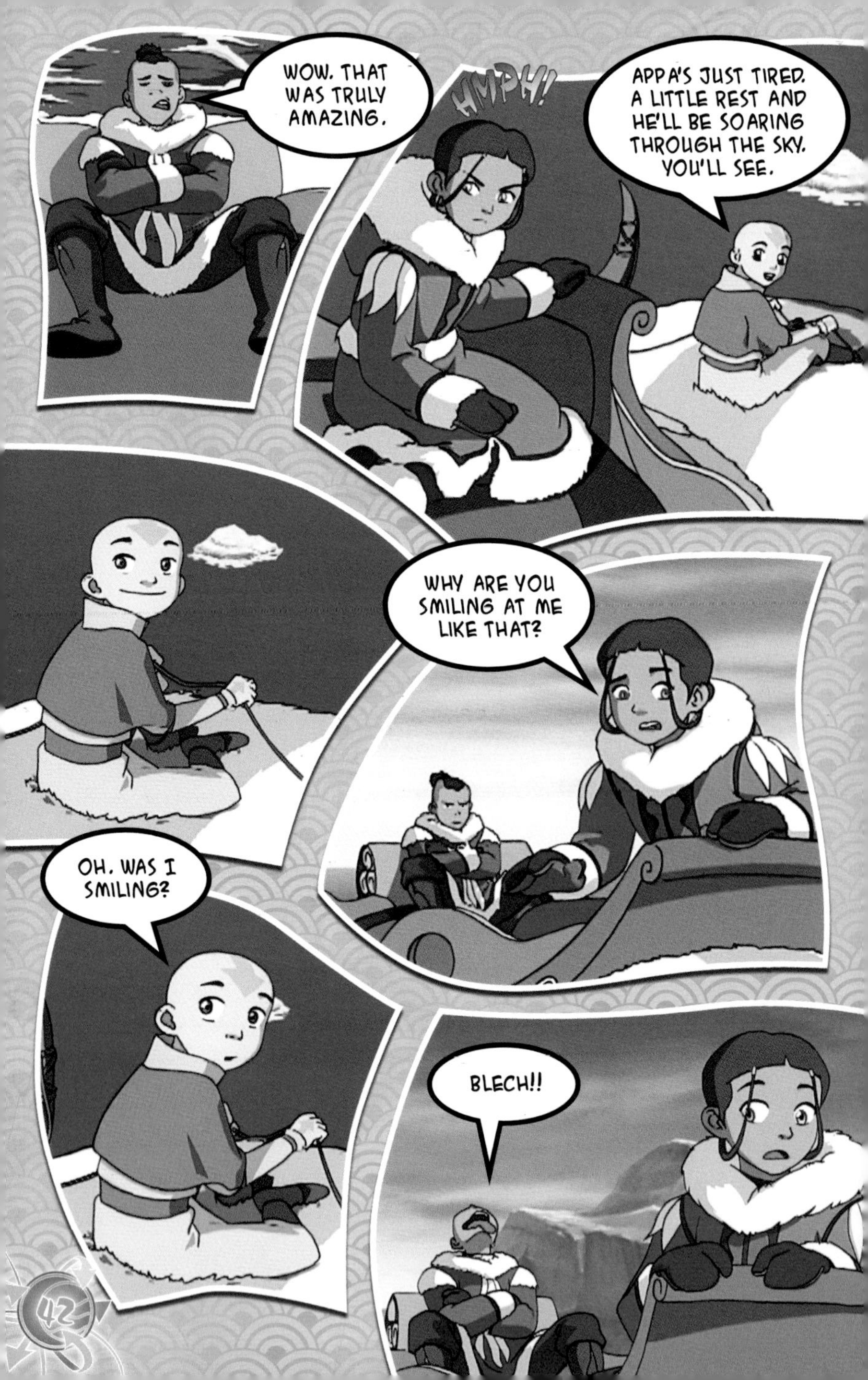
WOW. THAT WAS TRULY AMAZING.
HMPH!
APPA'S JUST TIRED. A LITTLE REST AND HE'LL BE SOARING THROUGH THE SKY. YOU'LL SEE.
WHY ARE YOU SMILING AT ME LIKE THAT?
OH. WAS I SMILING?
BLECH!!

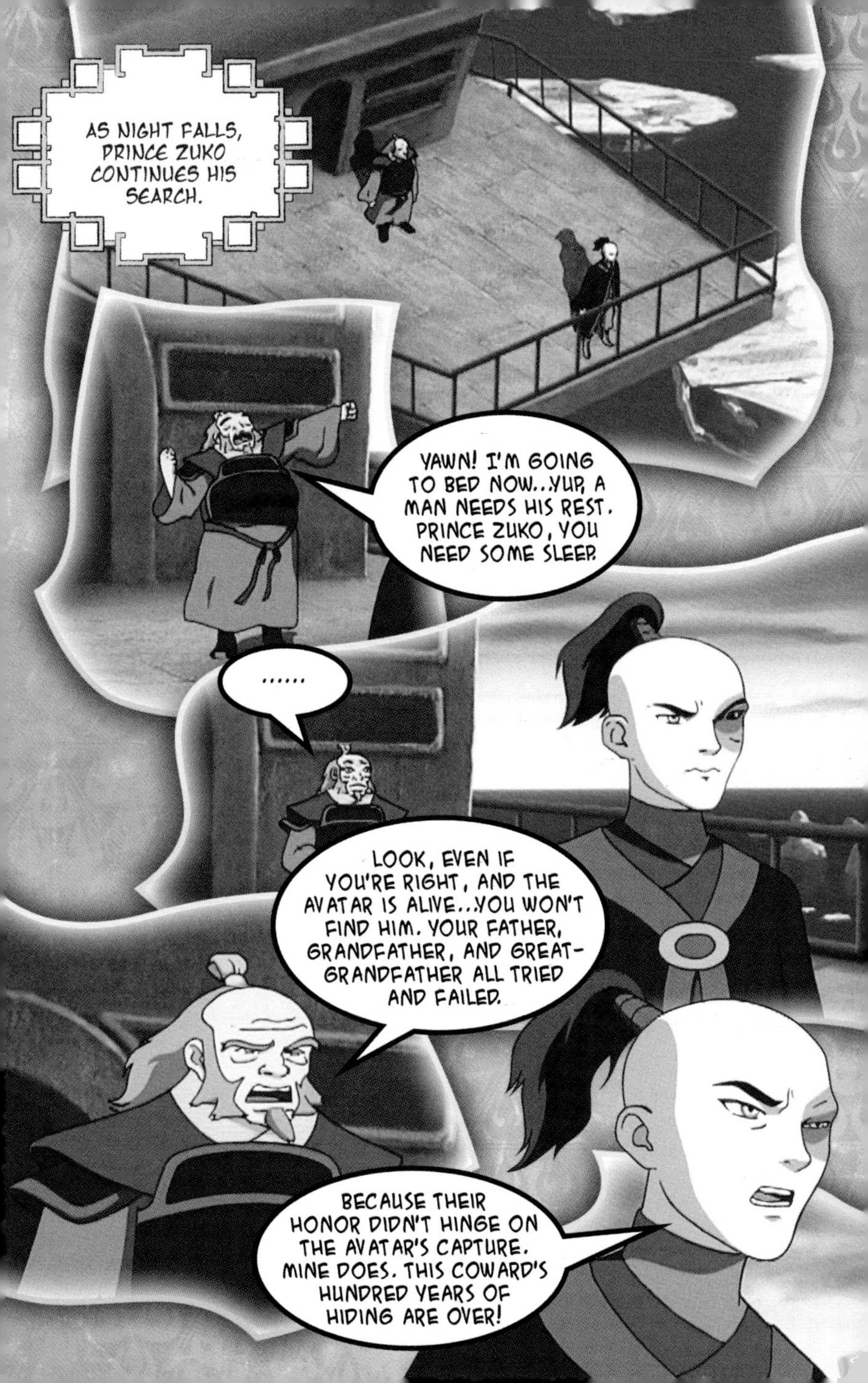
AS NIGHT FALLS, PRINCE ZUKO CONTINUES HIS SEARCH.
YAWN! I'M GOING TO BED NOW...YUP, A MAN NEEDS HIS REST. PRINCE ZUKO, YOU NEED SOME SLEEP.
......
LOOK, EVEN IF YOU'RE RIGHT, AND THE AVATAR IS ALIVE...YOU WON'T FIND HIM. YOUR FATHER, GRANDFATHER, AND GREAT-GRANDFATHER ALL TRIED AND FAILED.
BECAUSE THEIR HONOR DIDN'T HINGE ON THE AVATAR'S CAPTURE. MINE DOES. THIS COWARD'S HUNDRED YEARS OF HIDING ARE OVER!

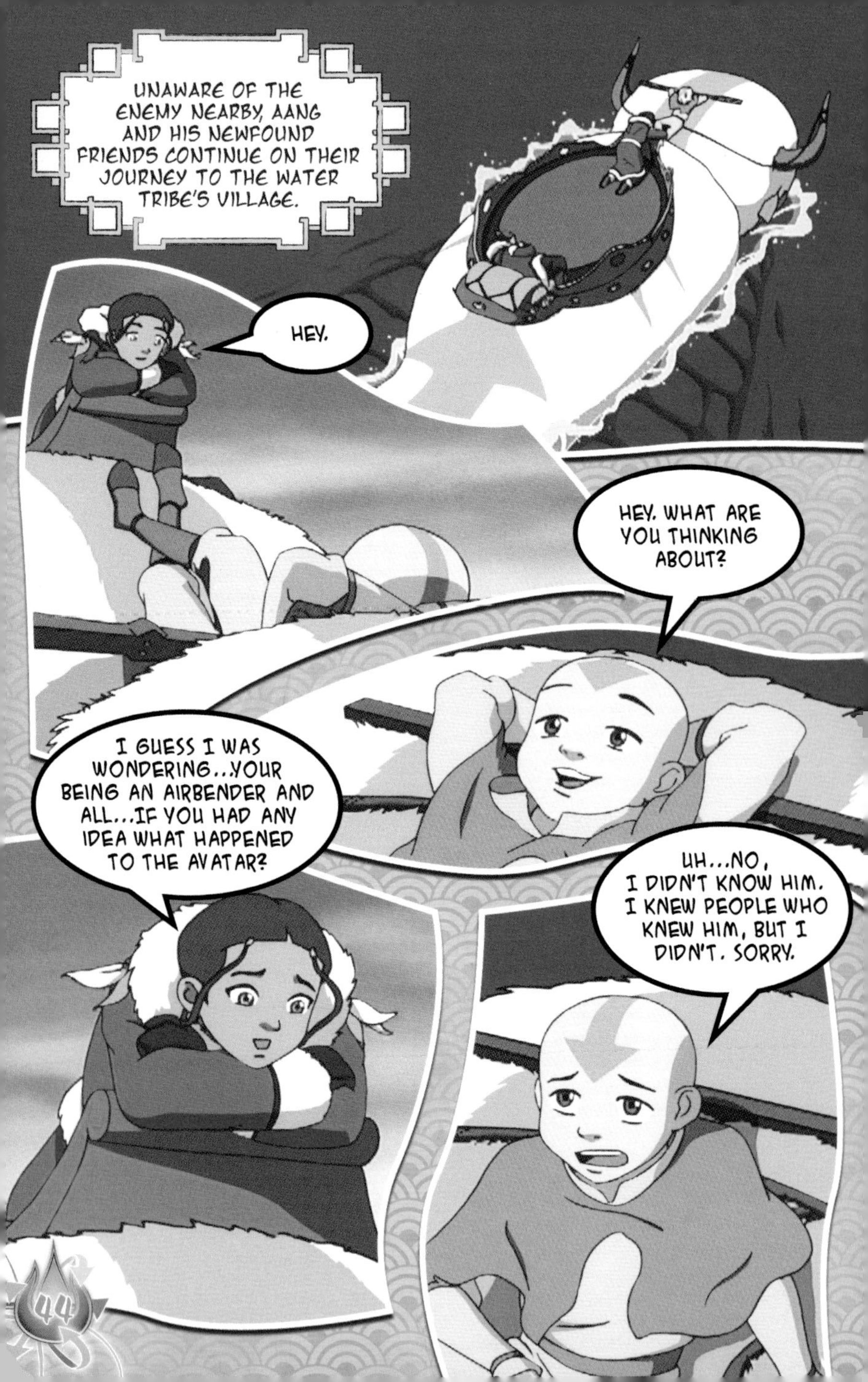
UNAWARE OF THE ENEMY NEARBY, AANG AND HIS NEWFOUND FRIENDS CONTINUE ON THEIR JOURNEY TO THE WATER TRIBE'S VILLAGE.
HEY.
HEY. WHAT ARE YOU THINKING ABOUT?
I GUESS I WAS WONDERING...YOUR BEING AN AIRBENDER AND ALL...IF YOU HAD ANY IDEA WHAT HAPPENED TO THE AVATAR?
UH...NO, I DIDN'T KNOW HIM. I KNEW PEOPLE WHO KNEW HIM, BUT I DIDN'T. SORRY.

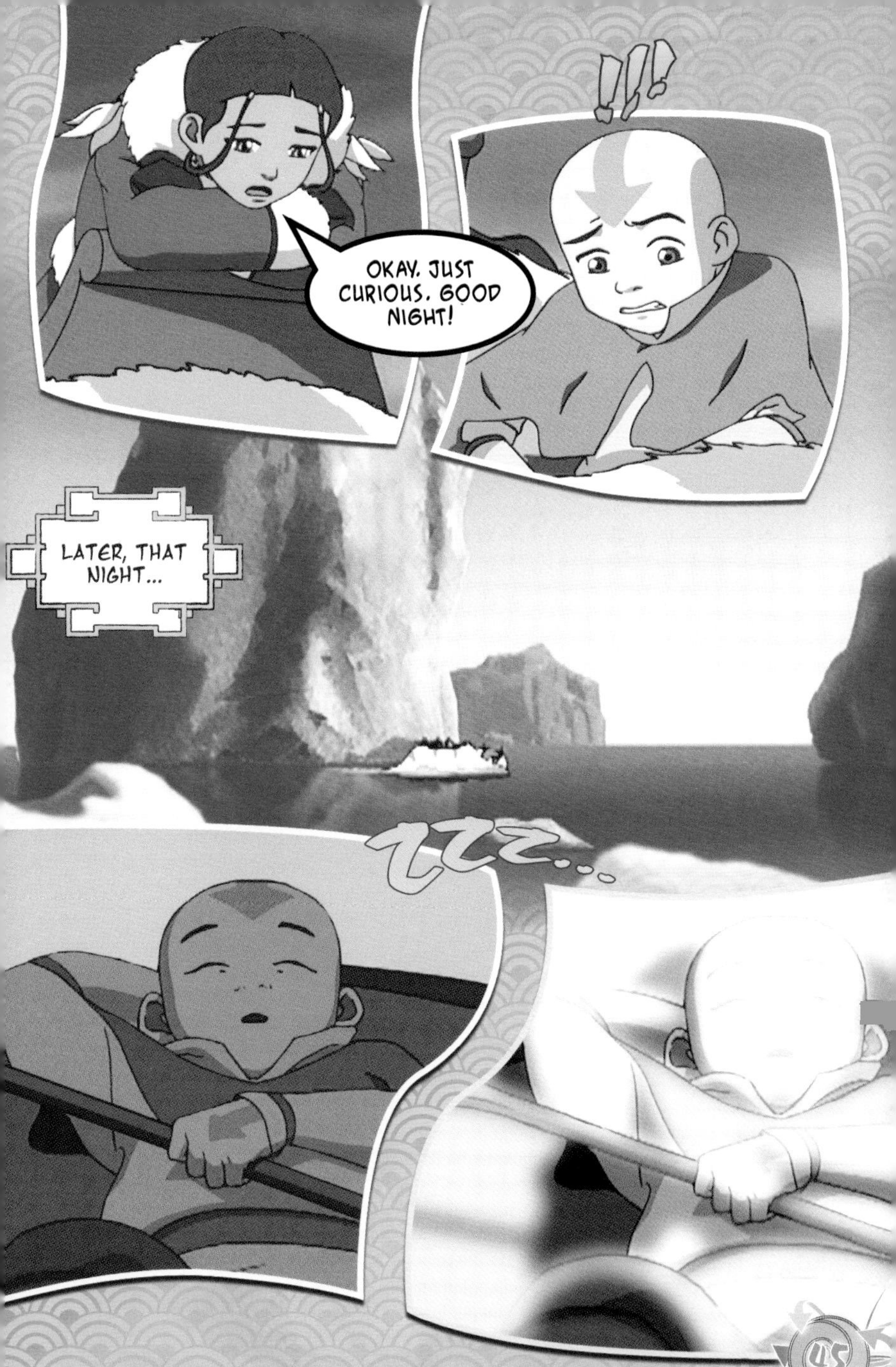
!!
OKAY. JUST CURIOUS. GOOD NIGHT!
LATER, THAT NIGHT...
ZZZ...

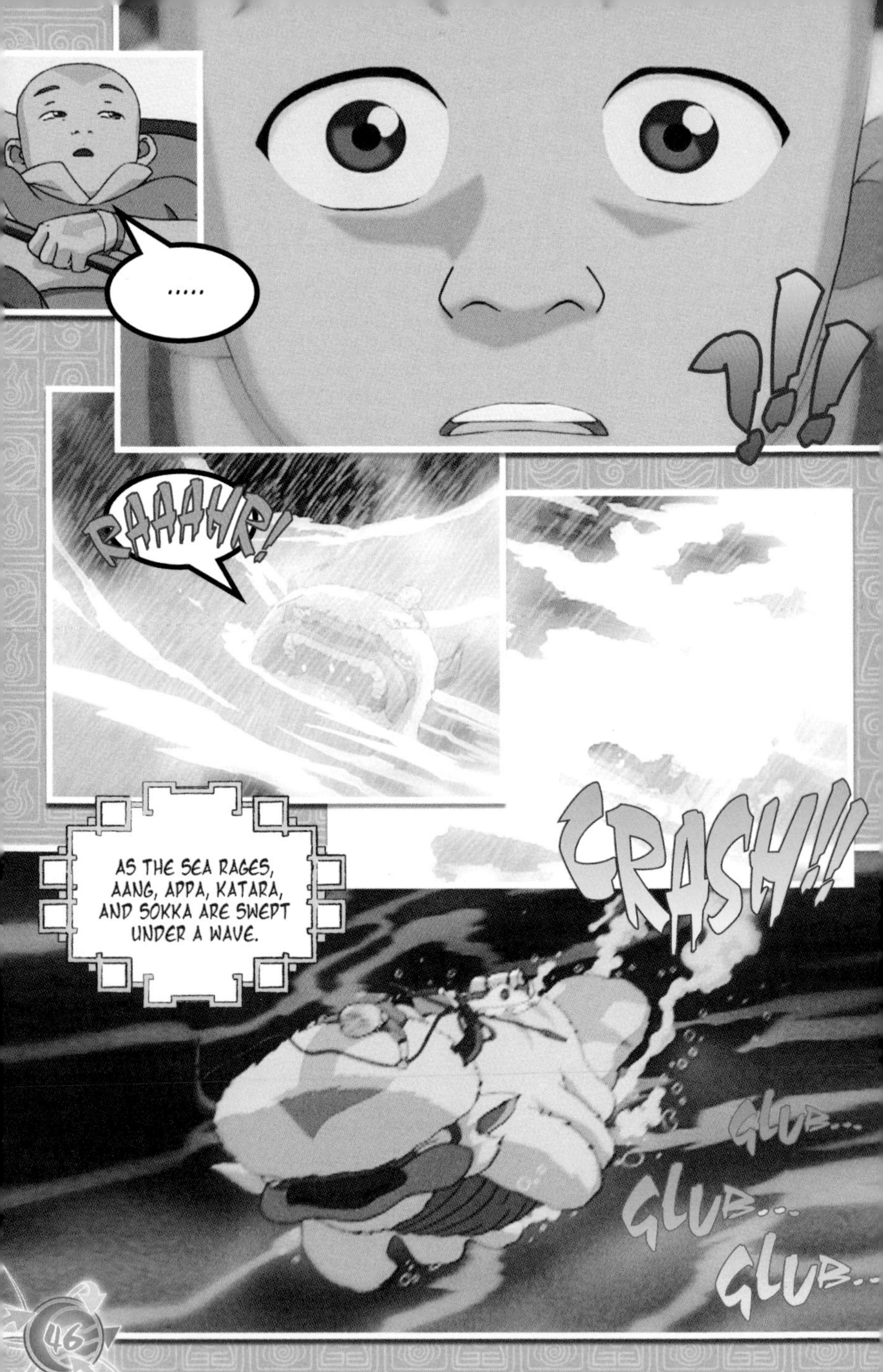
.....
!!!
RAAAHR!
CRASH!!
AS THE SEA RAGES, AANG, APPA, KATARA, AND SOKKA ARE SWEPT UNDER A WAVE.
GLUB...
GLUB...
GLUB...

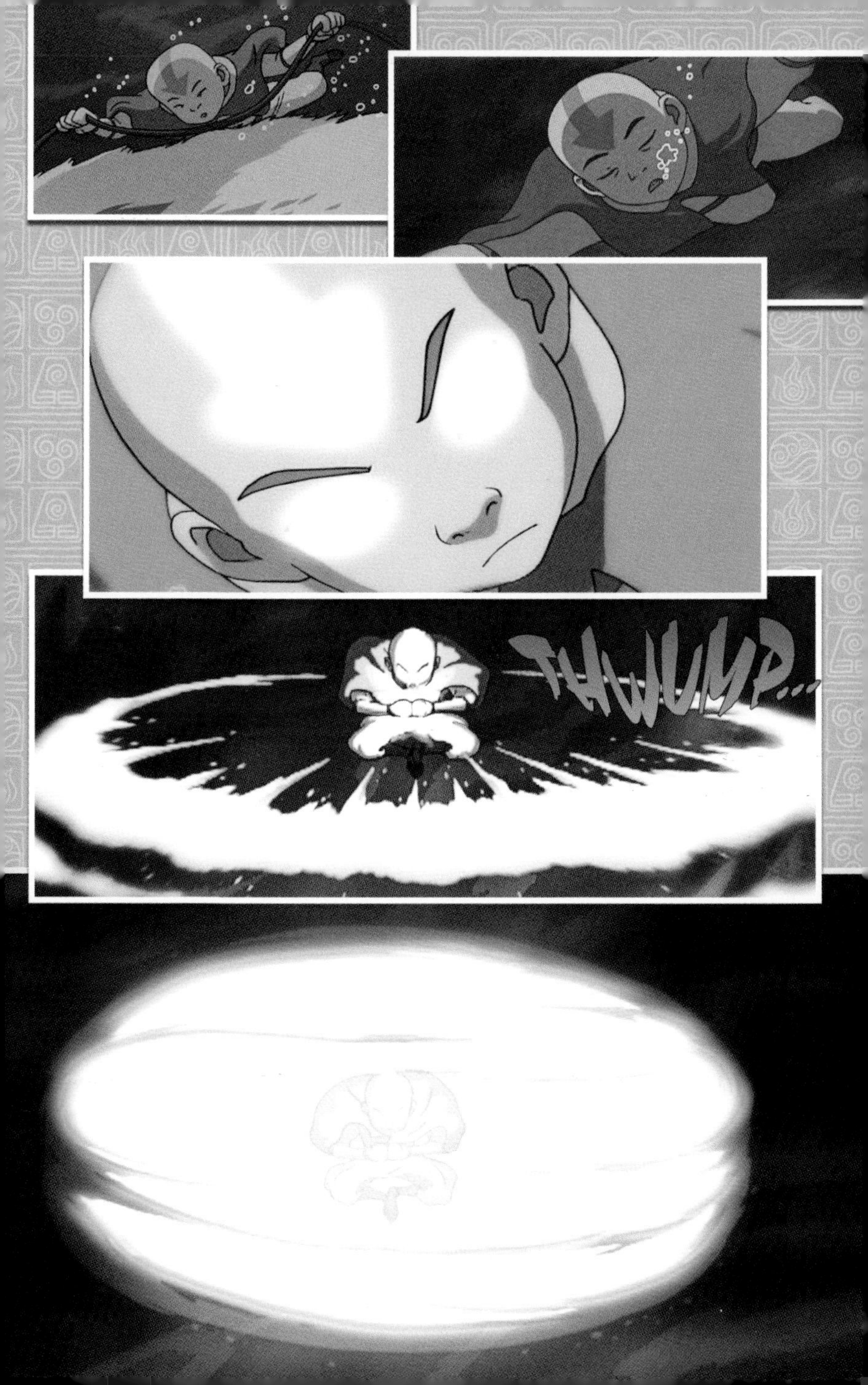
THWUMP...

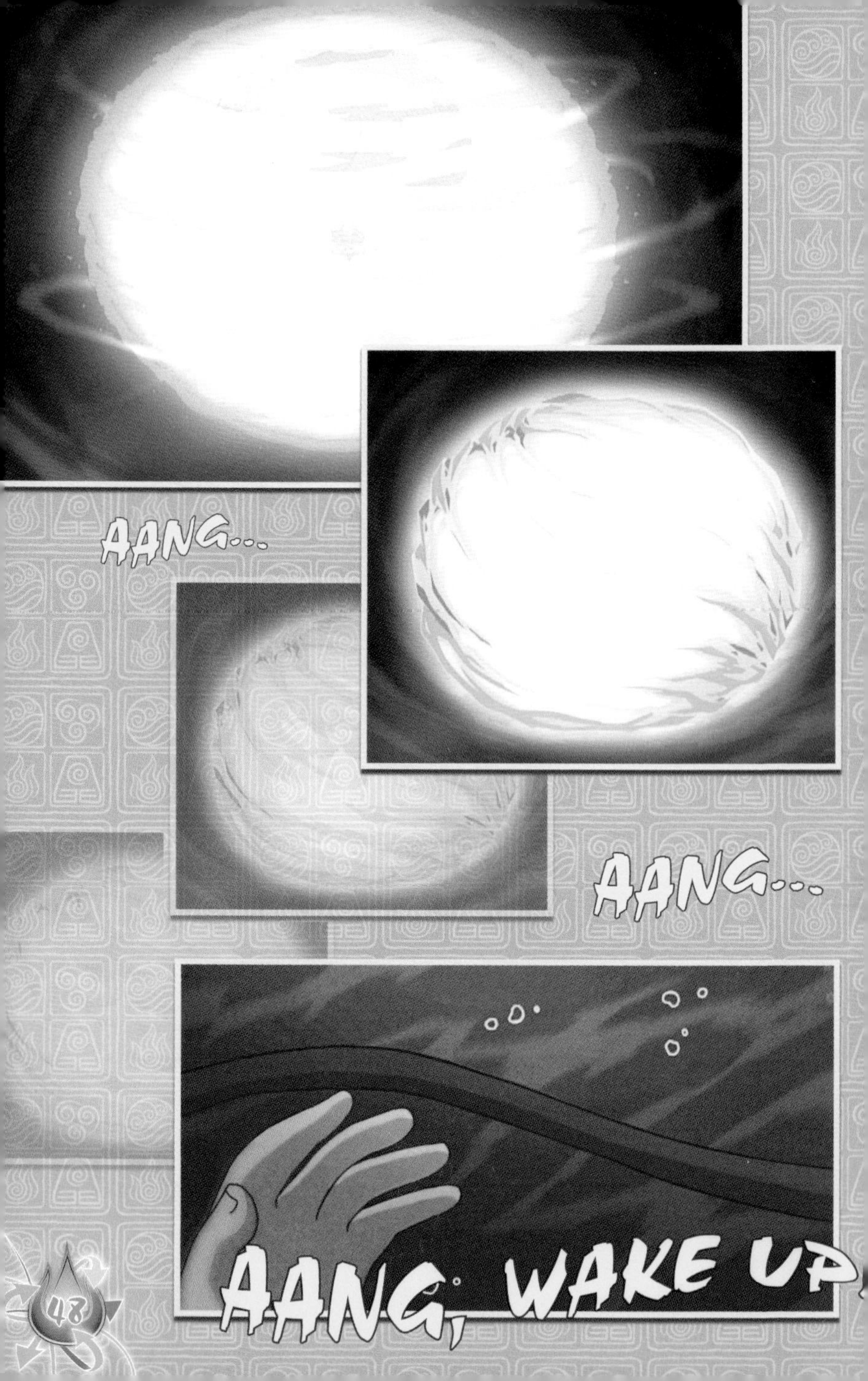
AANG...
AANG...
AANG, WAKE UP!

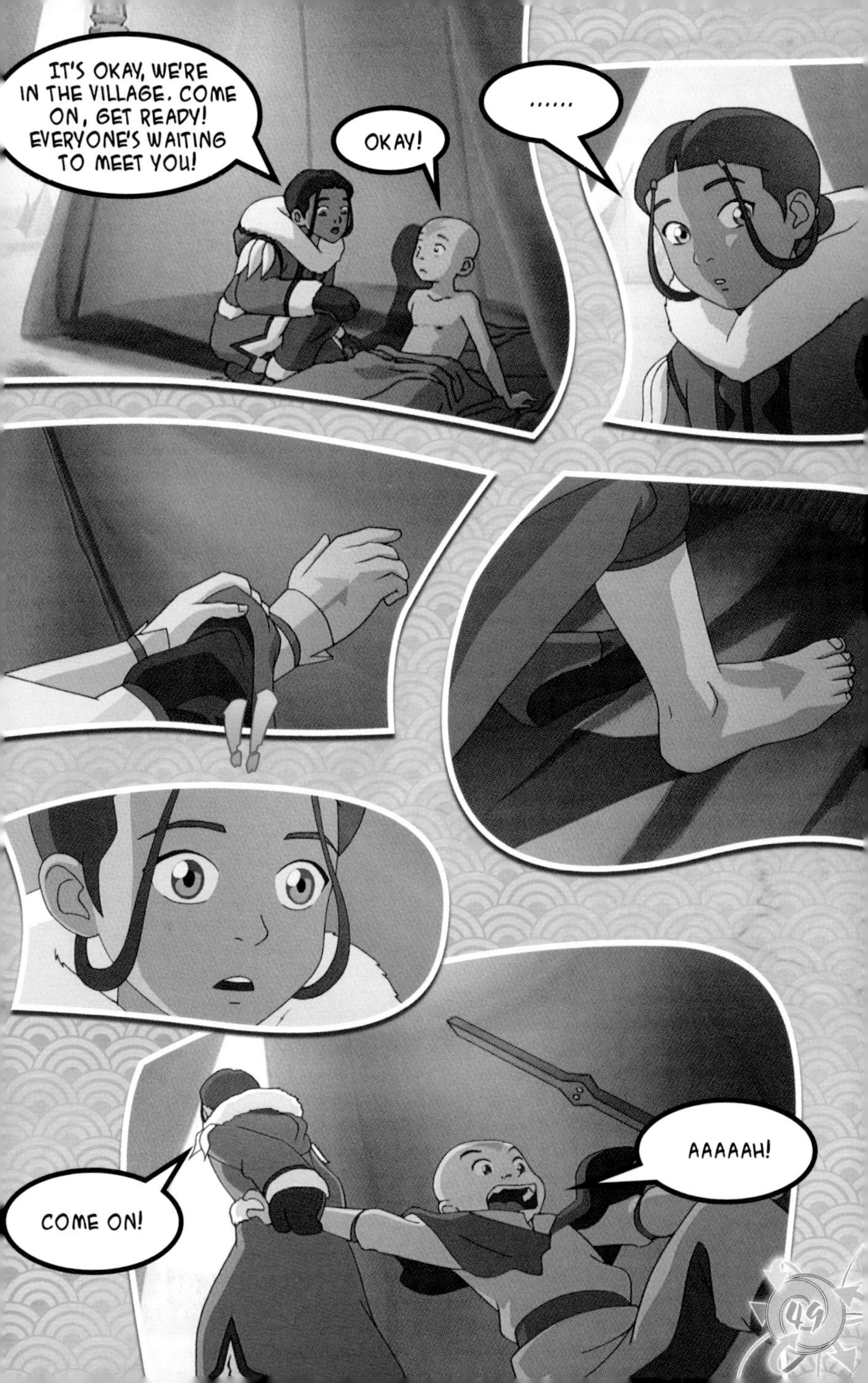
IT'S OKAY, WE'RE IN THE VILLAGE. COME ON, GET READY! EVERYONE'S WAITING TO MEET YOU!
OKAY!
......
COME ON!
AAAAAH!

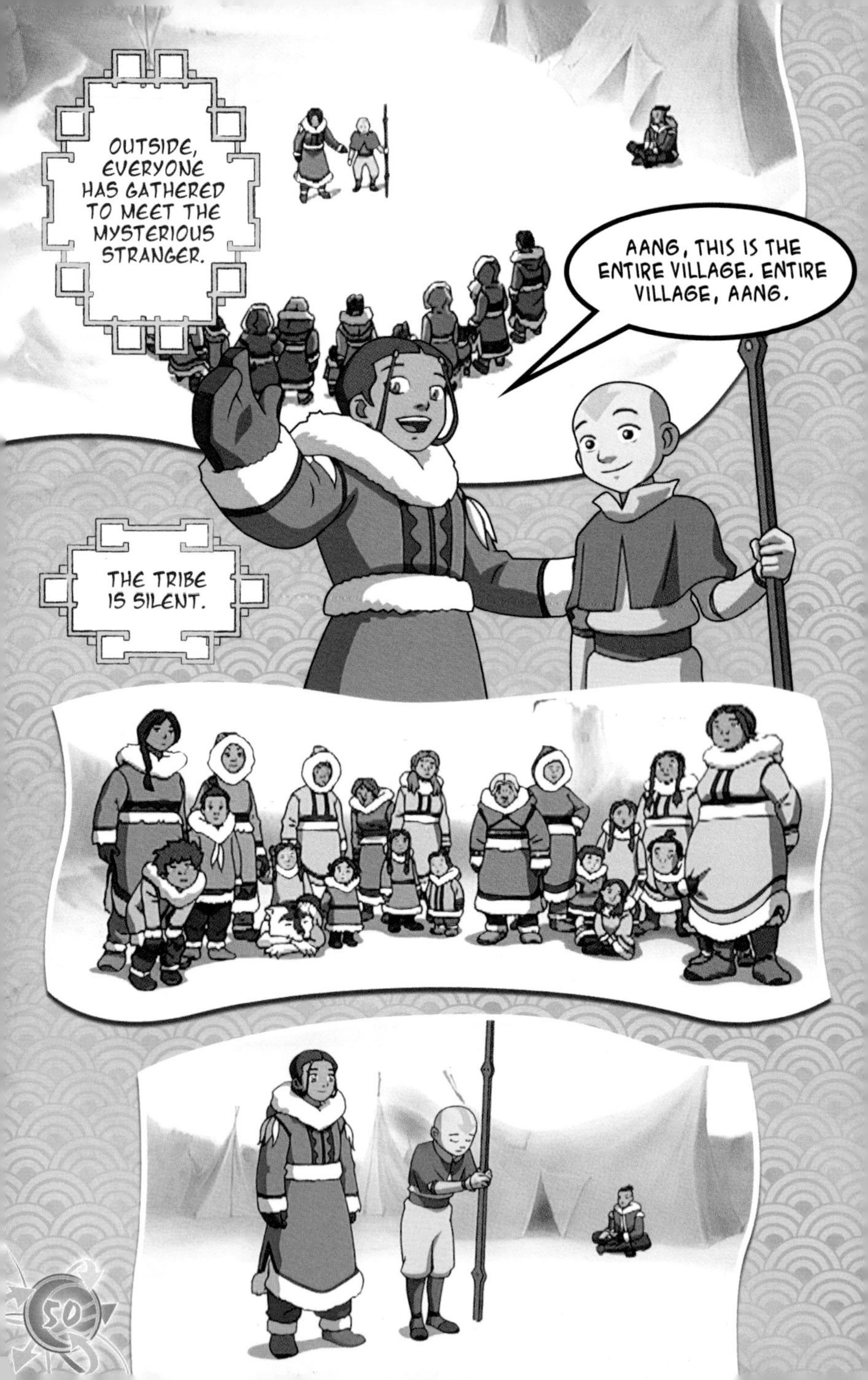
OUTSIDE, EVERYONE HAS GATHERED TO MEET THE MYSTERIOUS STRANGER.
AANG, THIS IS THE ENTIRE VILLAGE. ENTIRE VILLAGE, AANG.
THE TRIBE IS SILENT.

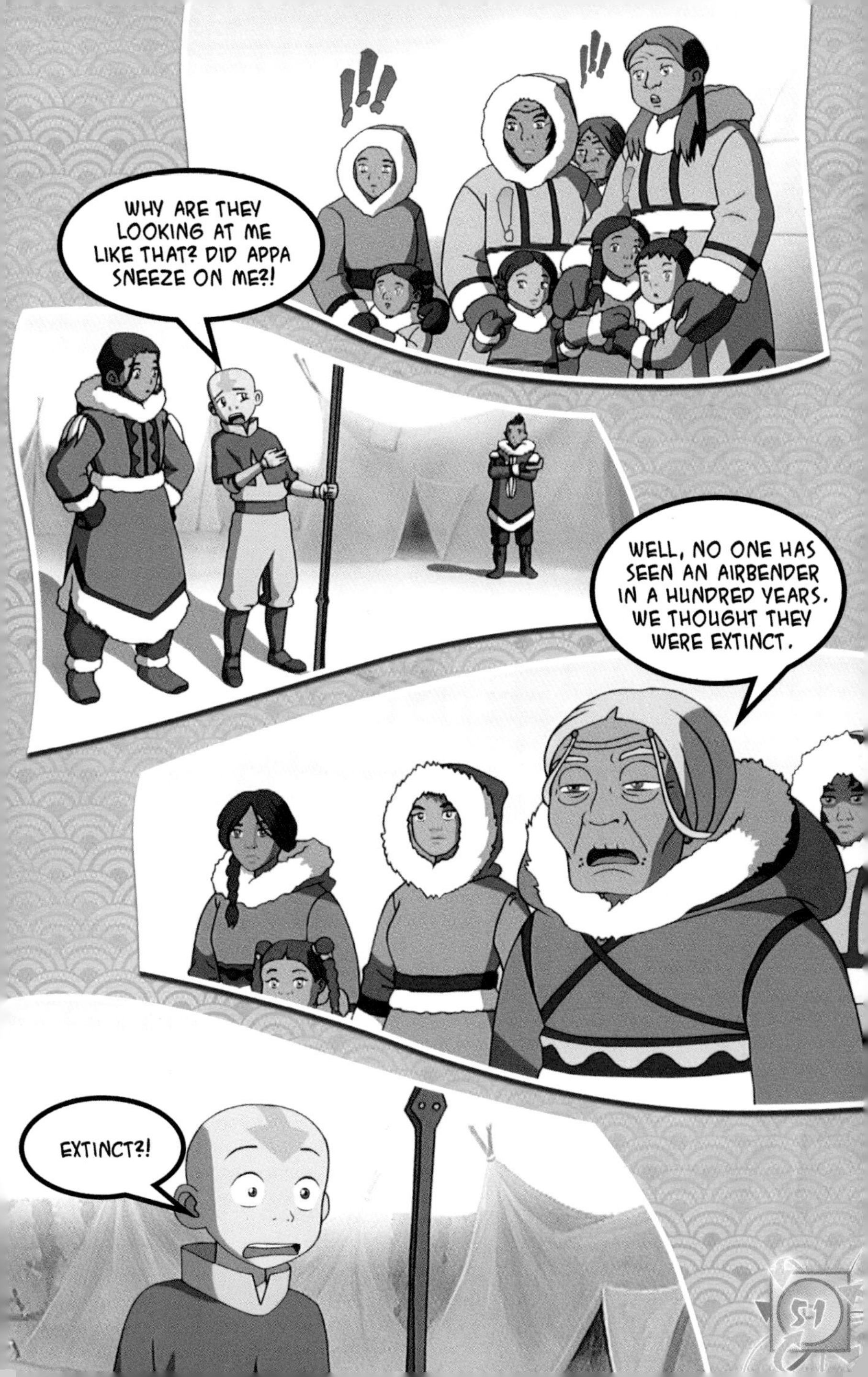
WHY ARE THEY LOOKING AT ME LIKE THAT? DID APPA SNEEZE ON ME?!
WELL, NO ONE HAS SEEN AN AIRBENDER IN A HUNDRED YEARS. WE THOUGHT THEY WERE EXTINCT.
EXTINCT?!

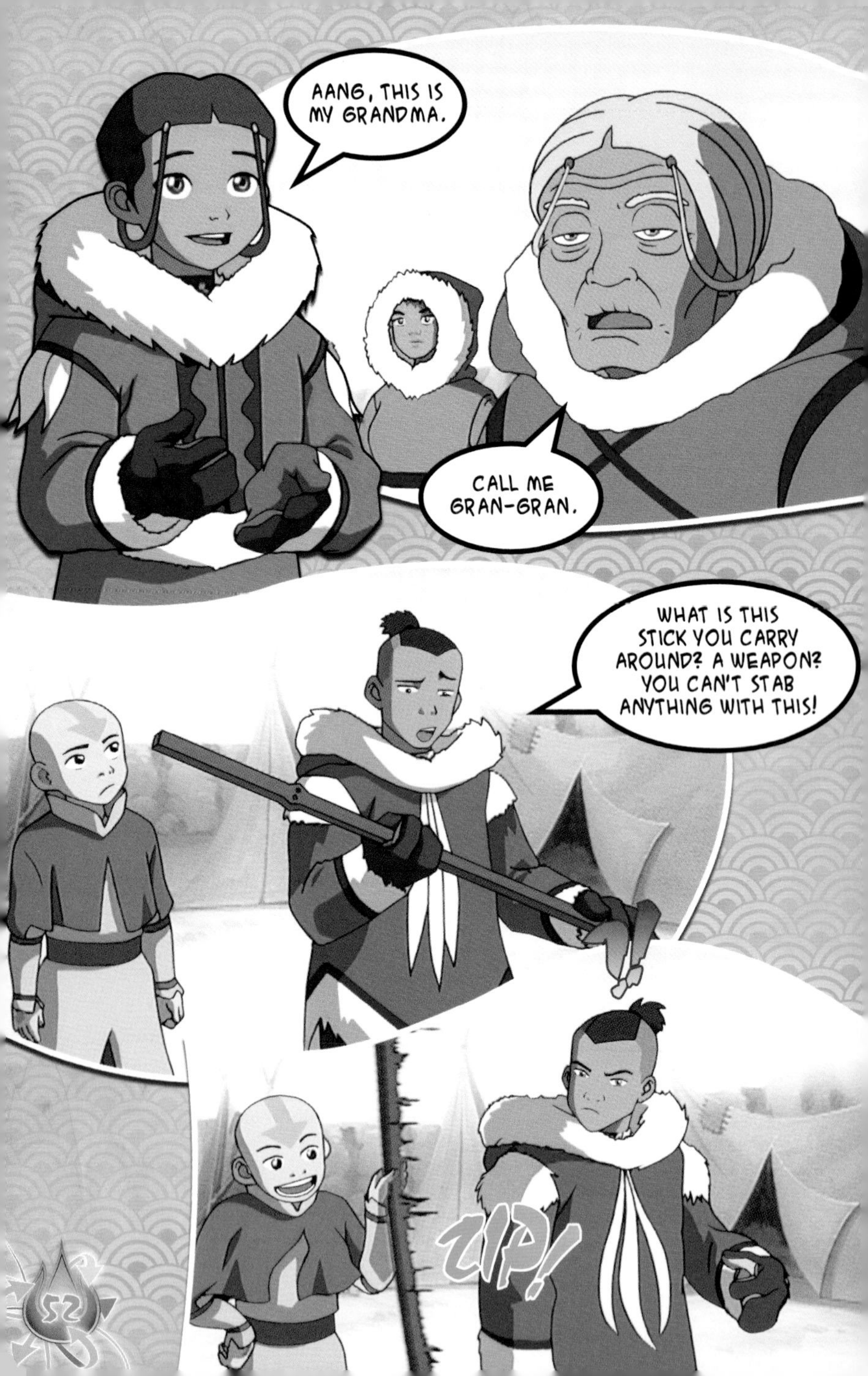
AANG, THIS IS MY GRANDMA.
CALL ME GRAN-GRAN.
WHAT IS THIS STICK YOU CARRY AROUND? A WEAPON? YOU CAN'T STAB ANYTHING WITH THIS!
ZIP!
52

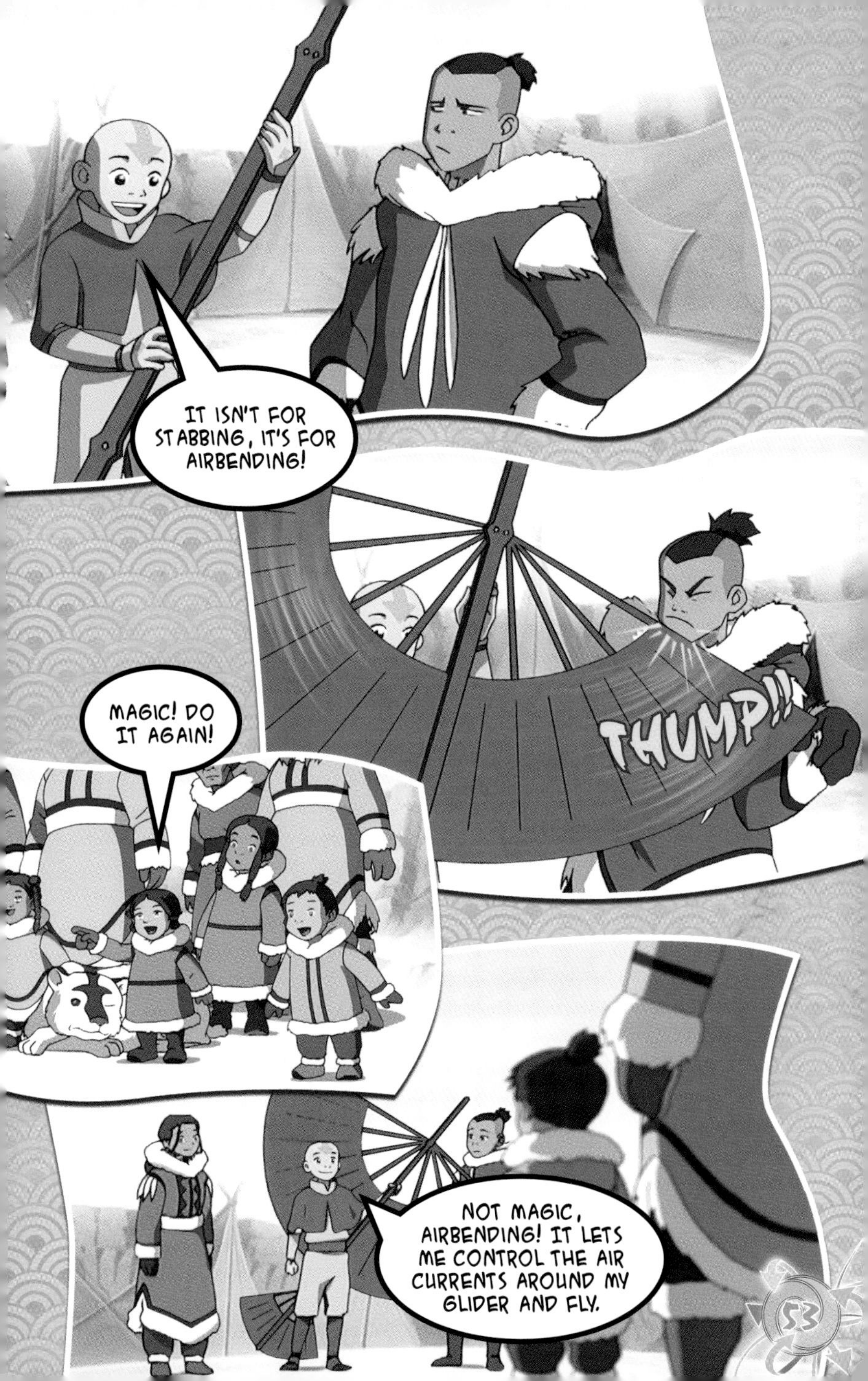
IT ISN'T FOR STABBING, IT'S FOR AIRBENDING!
THUMP!!
MAGIC! DO IT AGAIN!
NOT MAGIC, AIRBENDING! IT LETS ME CONTROL THE AIR CURRENTS AROUND MY GLIDER AND FLY.

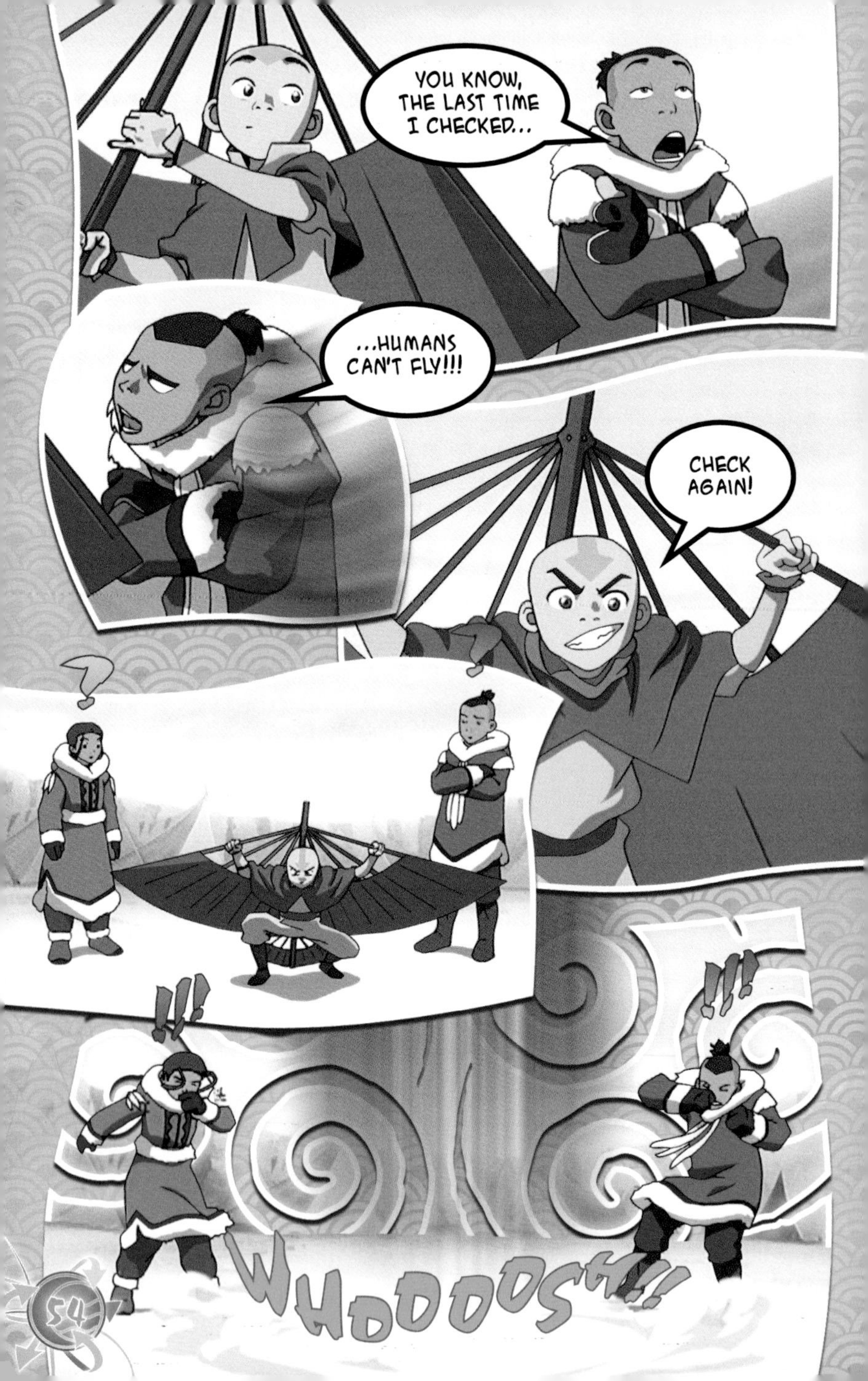
YOU KNOW, THE LAST TIME I CHECKED...
...HUMANS CAN'T FLY!!!
CHECK AGAIN!
?
!!
!!
WHOOOOSH!!

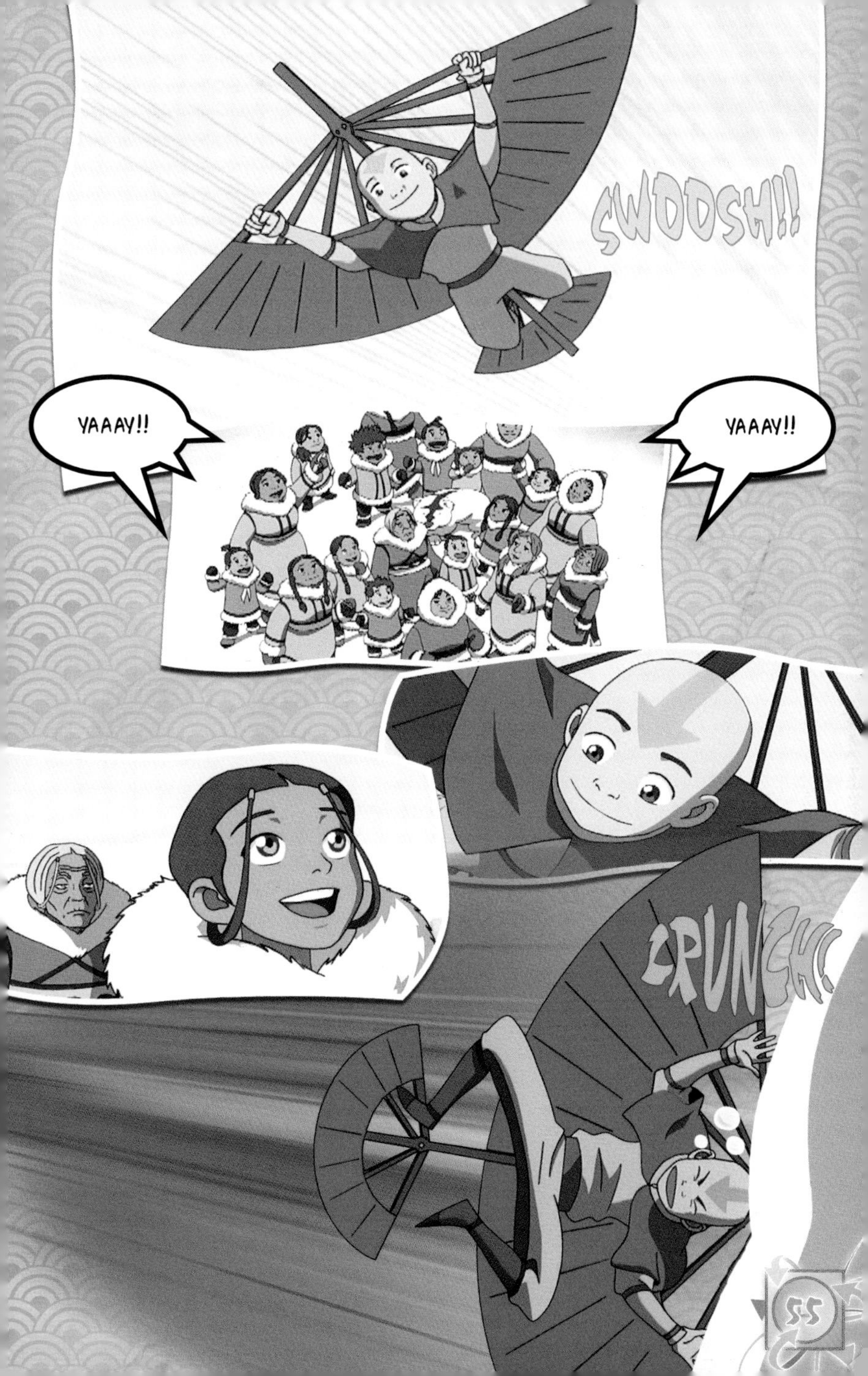
SWOOSH!!
YAAAY!!
YAAAY!!
CRUNCH!

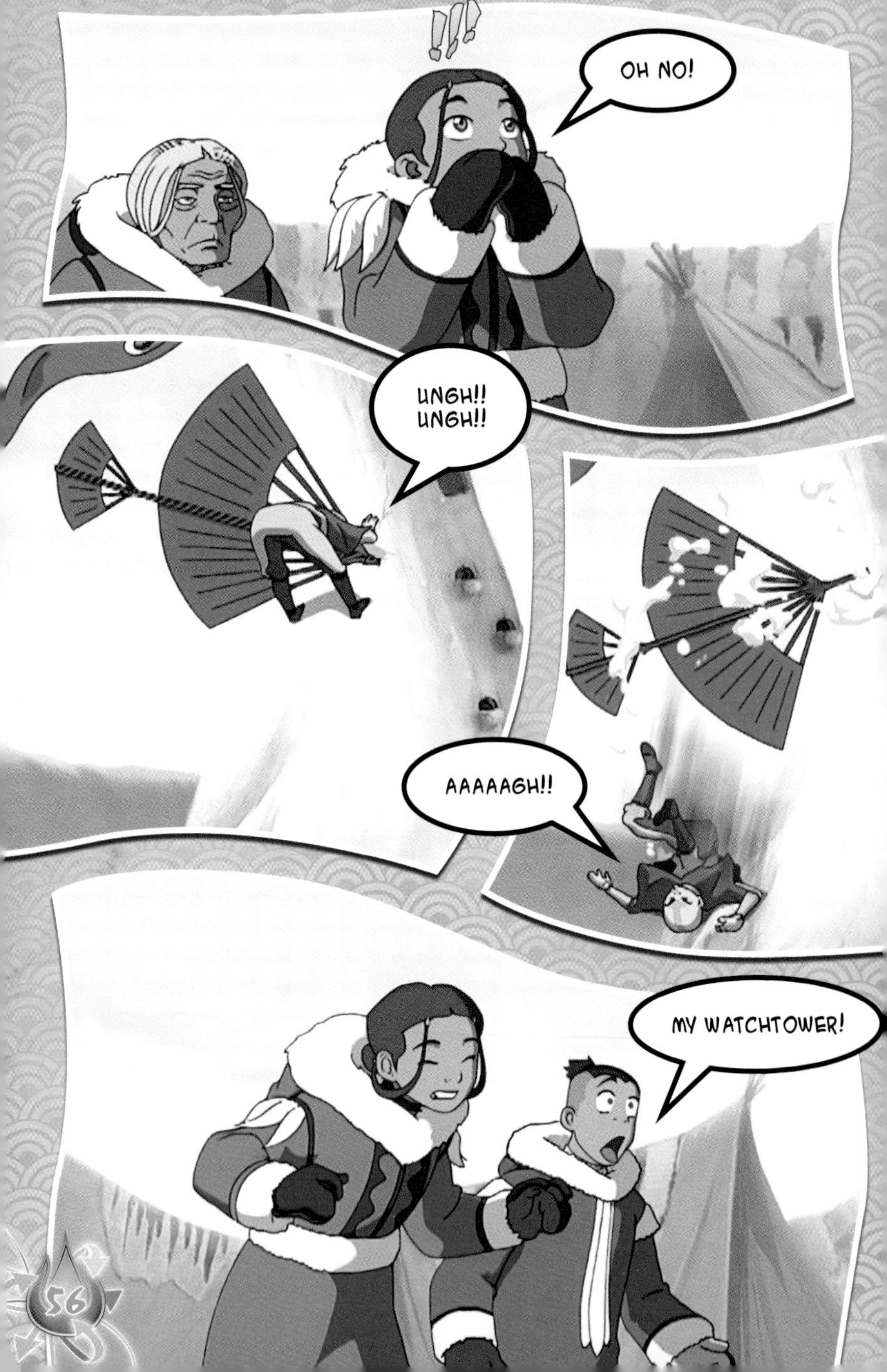

OH NO!
UNGH!! UNGH!!
AAAAAGH!!
MY WATCHTOWER!

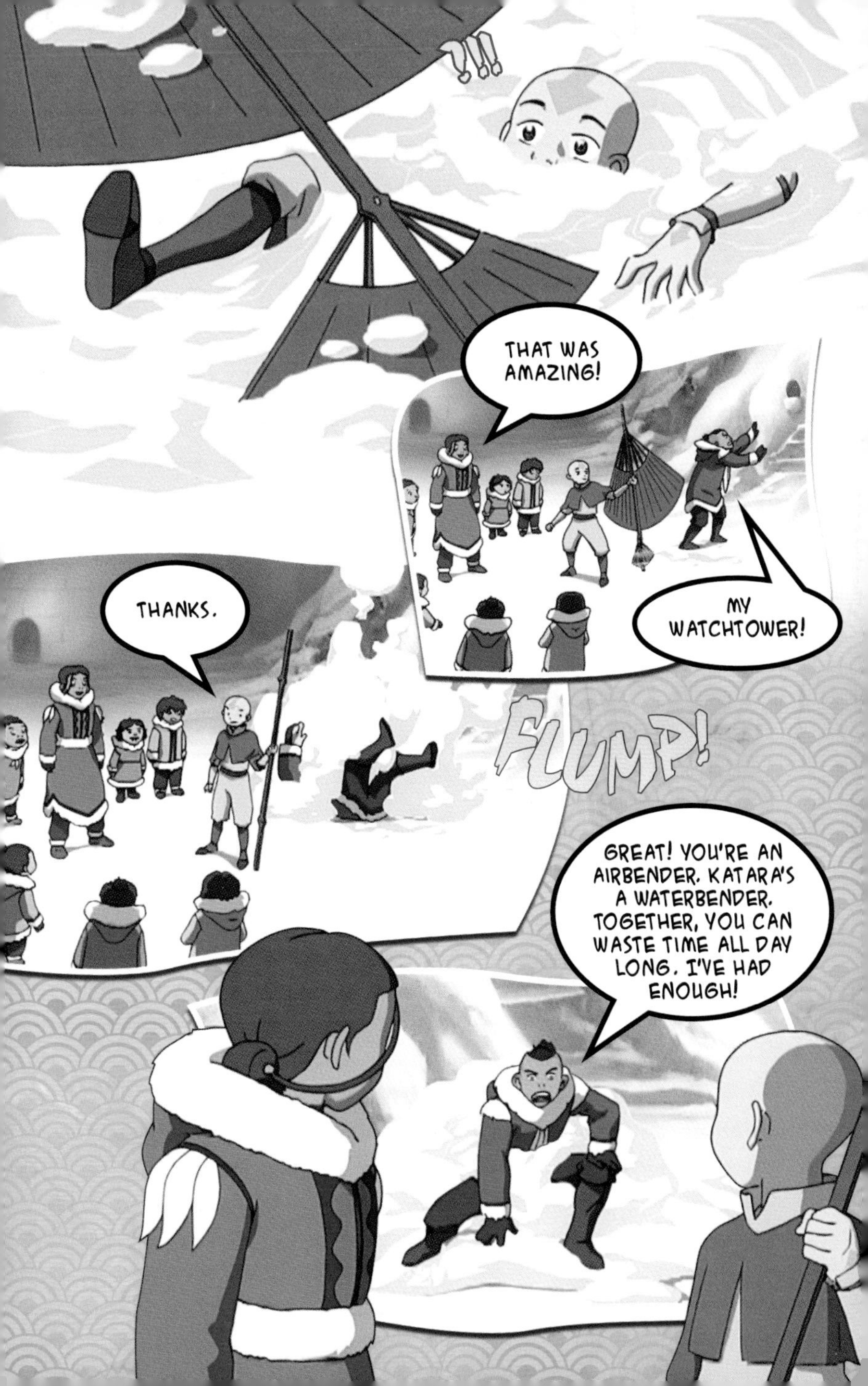
?!!
THAT WAS AMAZING!
MY WATCHTOWER!
THANKS.
FLUMP!
GREAT! YOU'RE AN AIRBENDER. KATARA'S A WATERBENDER. TOGETHER, YOU CAN WASTE TIME ALL DAY LONG. I'VE HAD ENOUGH!

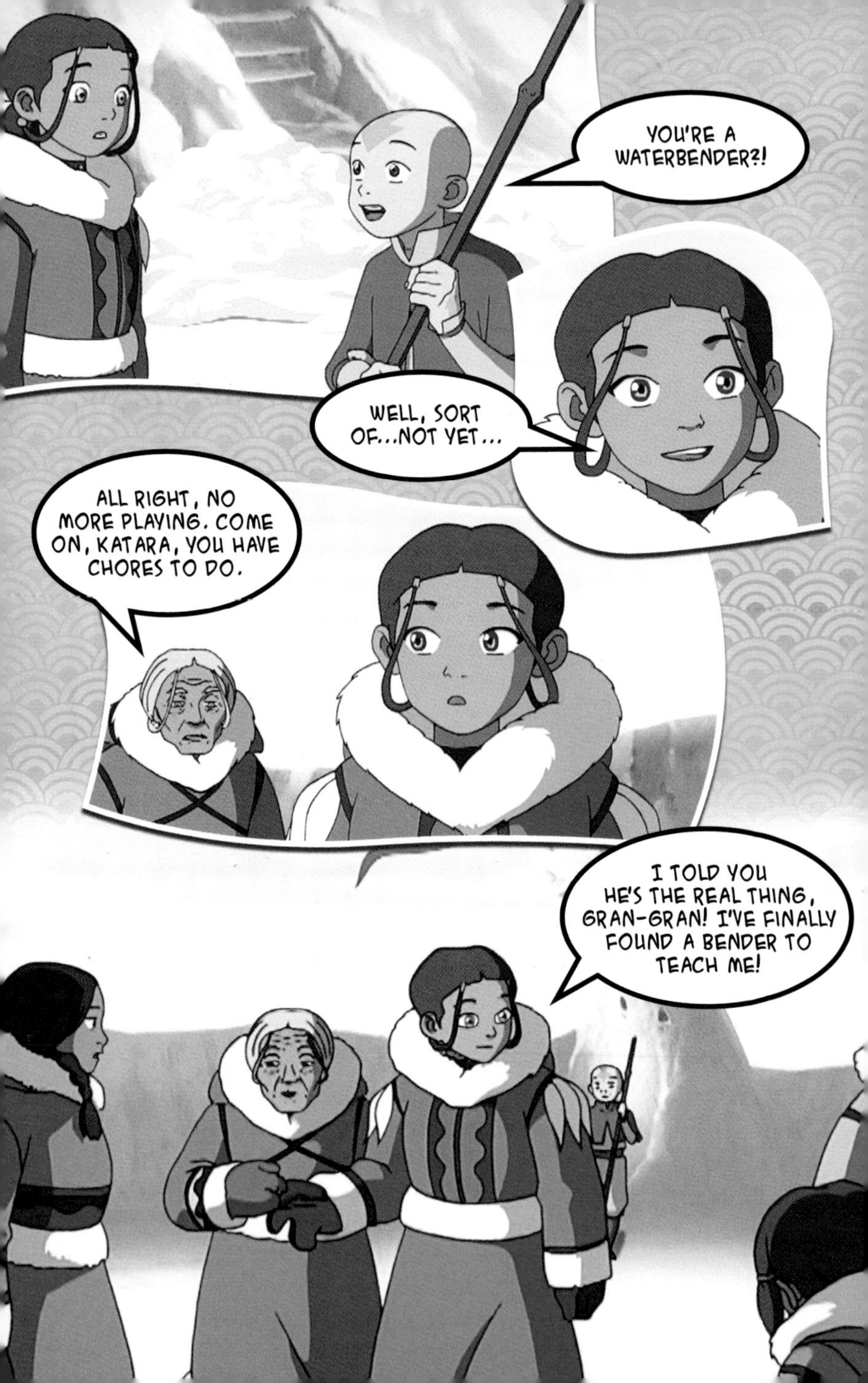
YOU'RE A WATERBENDER?!
WELL, SORT OF...NOT YET...
ALL RIGHT, NO MORE PLAYING. COME ON, KATARA, YOU HAVE CHORES TO DO.
I TOLD YOU HE'S THE REAL THING, GRAN-GRAN! I'VE FINALLY FOUND A BENDER TO TEACH ME!

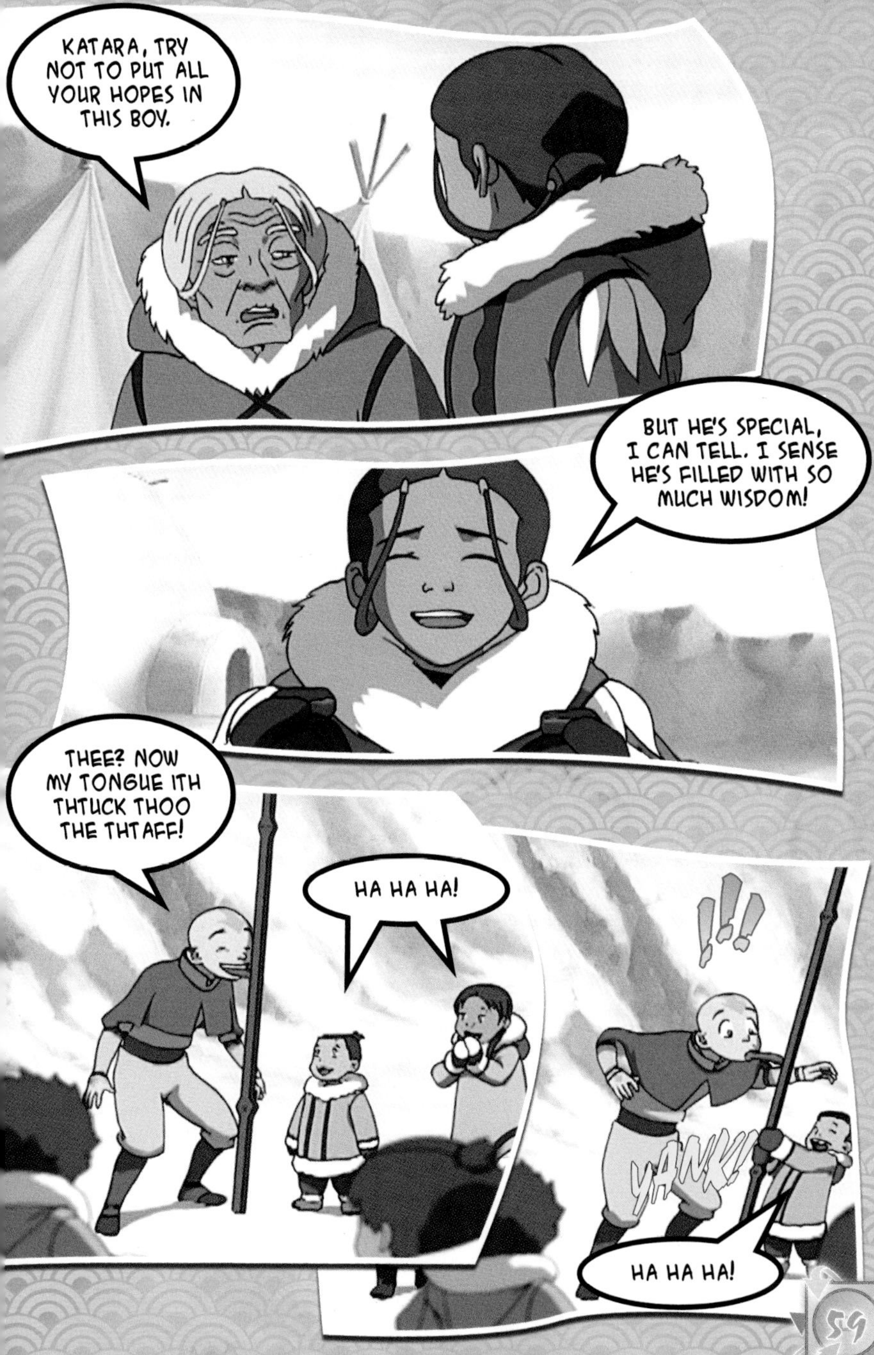
KATARA, TRY NOT TO PUT ALL YOUR HOPES IN THIS BOY.
BUT HE'S SPECIAL, I CAN TELL. I SENSE HE'S FILLED WITH SO MUCH WISDOM!
THEE? NOW MY TONGUE ITH THTUCK THOO THE THTAFF!
HA HA HA!
!!!
YANK!
HA HA HA!

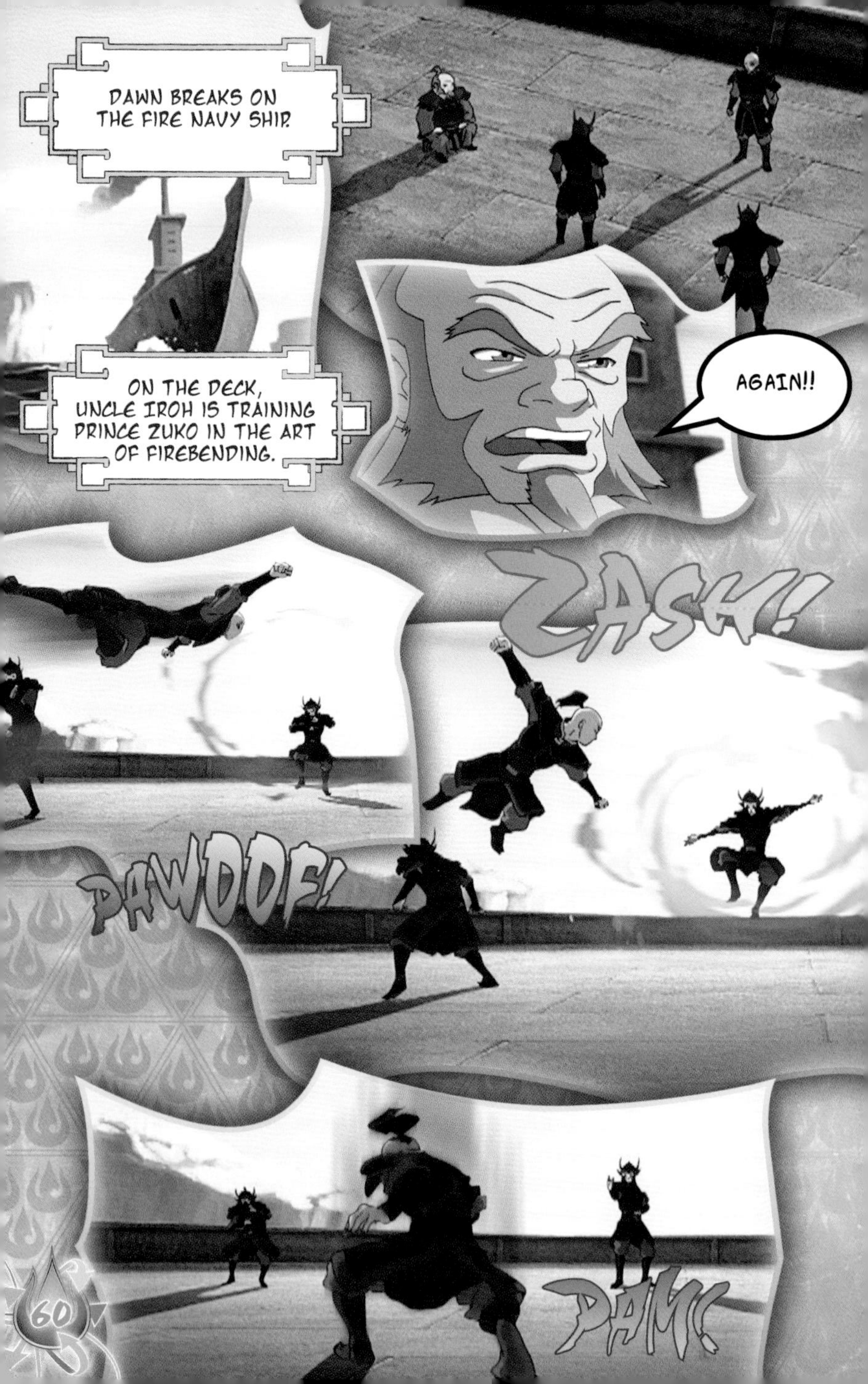
DAWN BREAKS ON THE FIRE NAVY SHIP.
ON THE DECK, UNCLE IROH IS TRAINING PRINCE ZUKO IN THE ART OF FIREBENDING.
AGAIN!!
ZASH!
PAWOOF!
PAM!

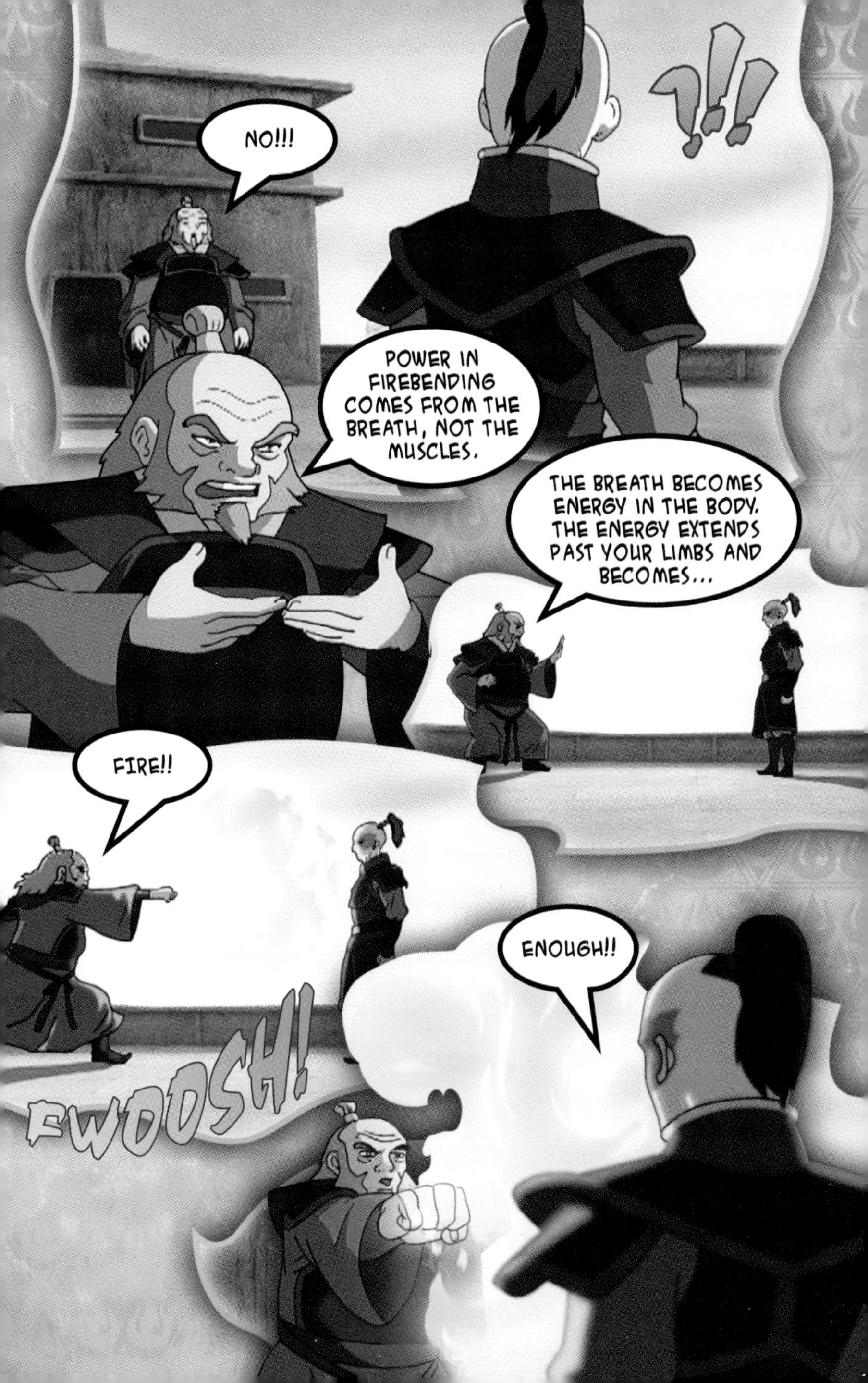
NO!!!
?!!
POWER IN FIREBENDING COMES FROM THE BREATH, NOT THE MUSCLES.
THE BREATH BECOMES ENERGY IN THE BODY. THE ENERGY EXTENDS PAST YOUR LIMBS AND BECOMES...
FIRE!!
FWOOSH!
ENOUGH!!

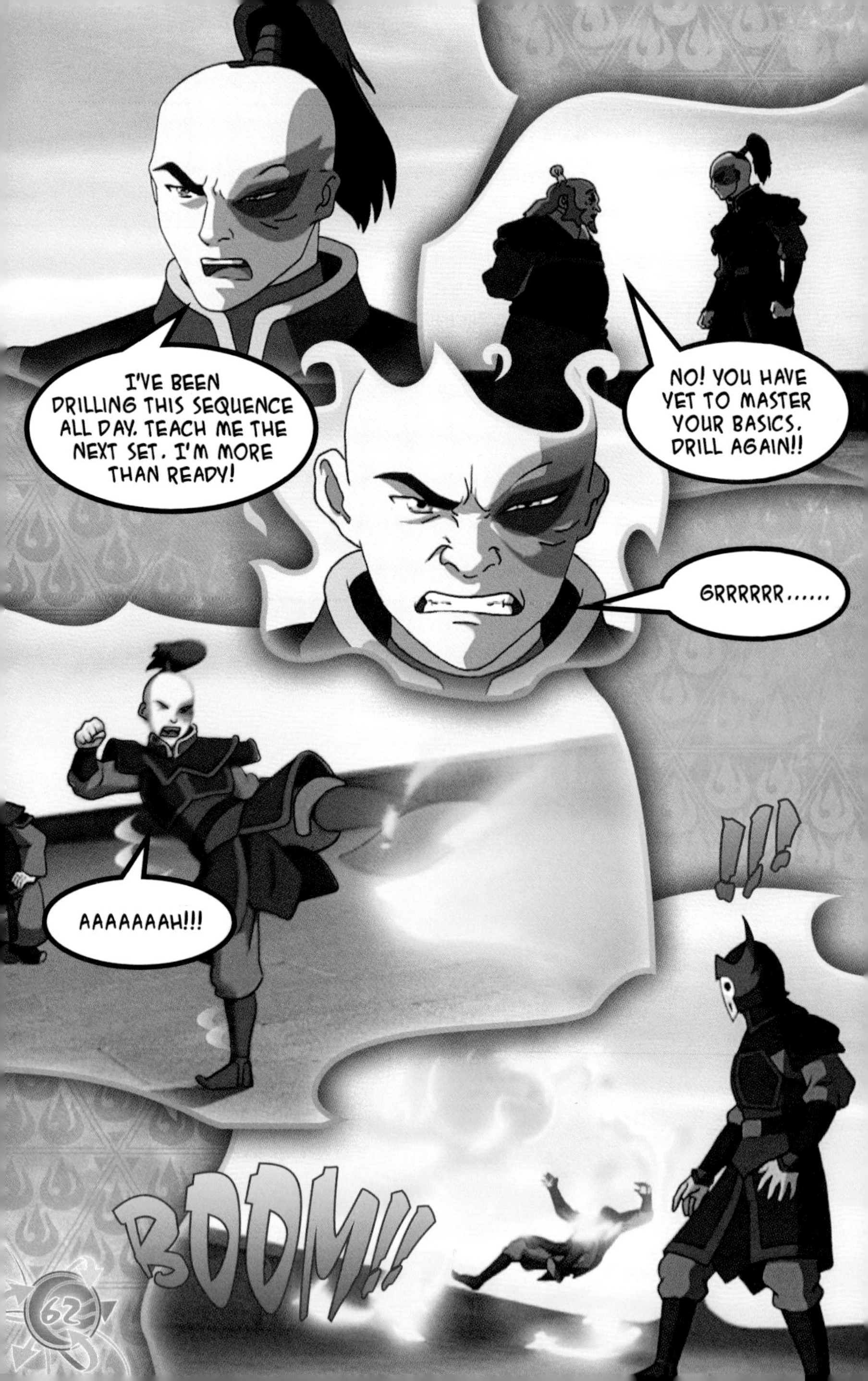
I'VE BEEN DRILLING THIS SEQUENCE ALL DAY. TEACH ME THE NEXT SET. I'M MORE THAN READY!
NO! YOU HAVE YET TO MASTER YOUR BASICS. DRILL AGAIN!!
GRRRRRR......
AAAAAAAH!!!
!!!
BOOM!!

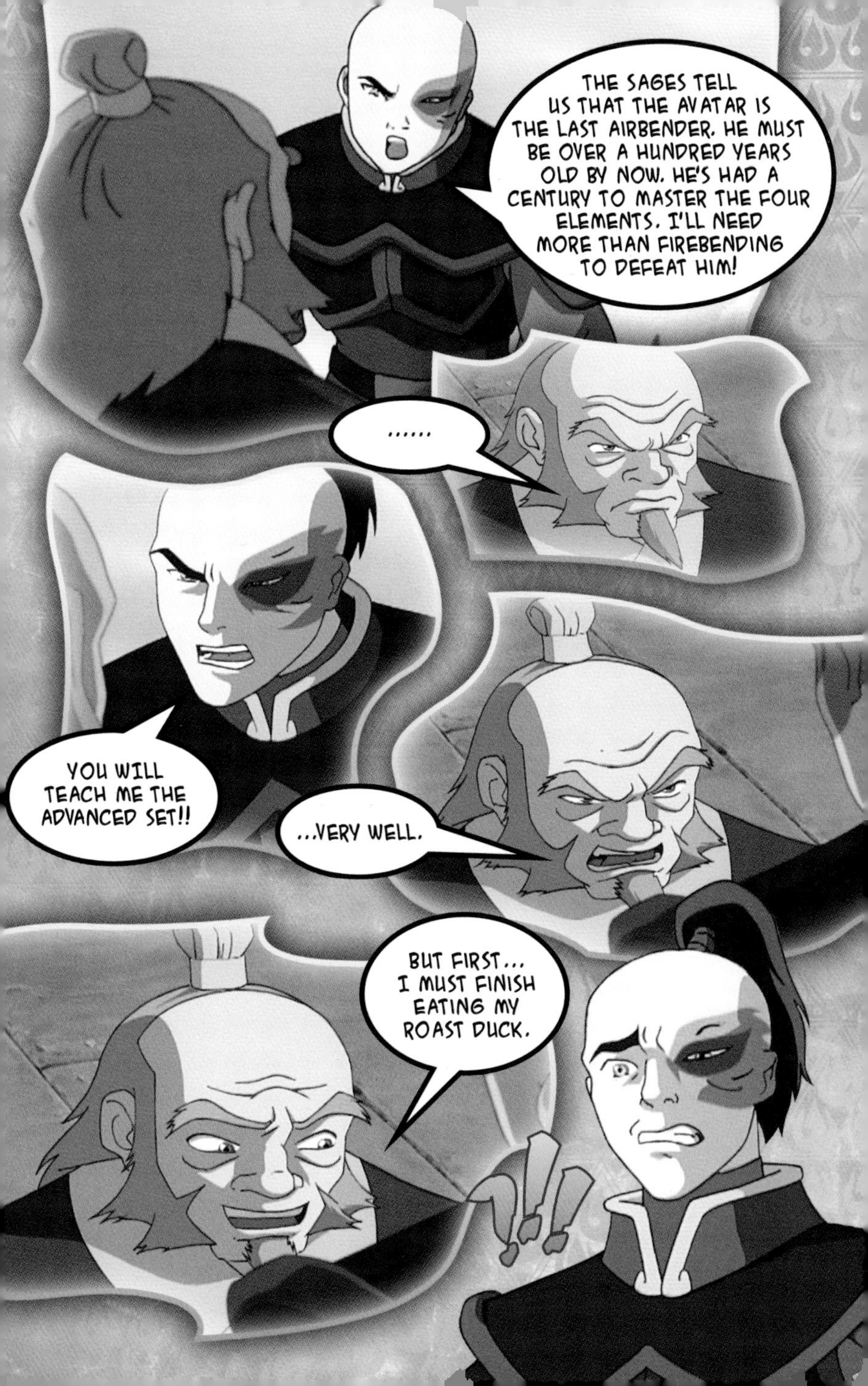
THE SAGES TELL US THAT THE AVATAR IS THE LAST AIRBENDER. HE MUST BE OVER A HUNDRED YEARS OLD BY NOW. HE'S HAD A CENTURY TO MASTER THE FOUR ELEMENTS. I'LL NEED MORE THAN FIREBENDING TO DEFEAT HIM!
......
YOU WILL TEACH ME THE ADVANCED SET!!
...VERY WELL.
BUT FIRST... I MUST FINISH EATING MY ROAST DUCK.

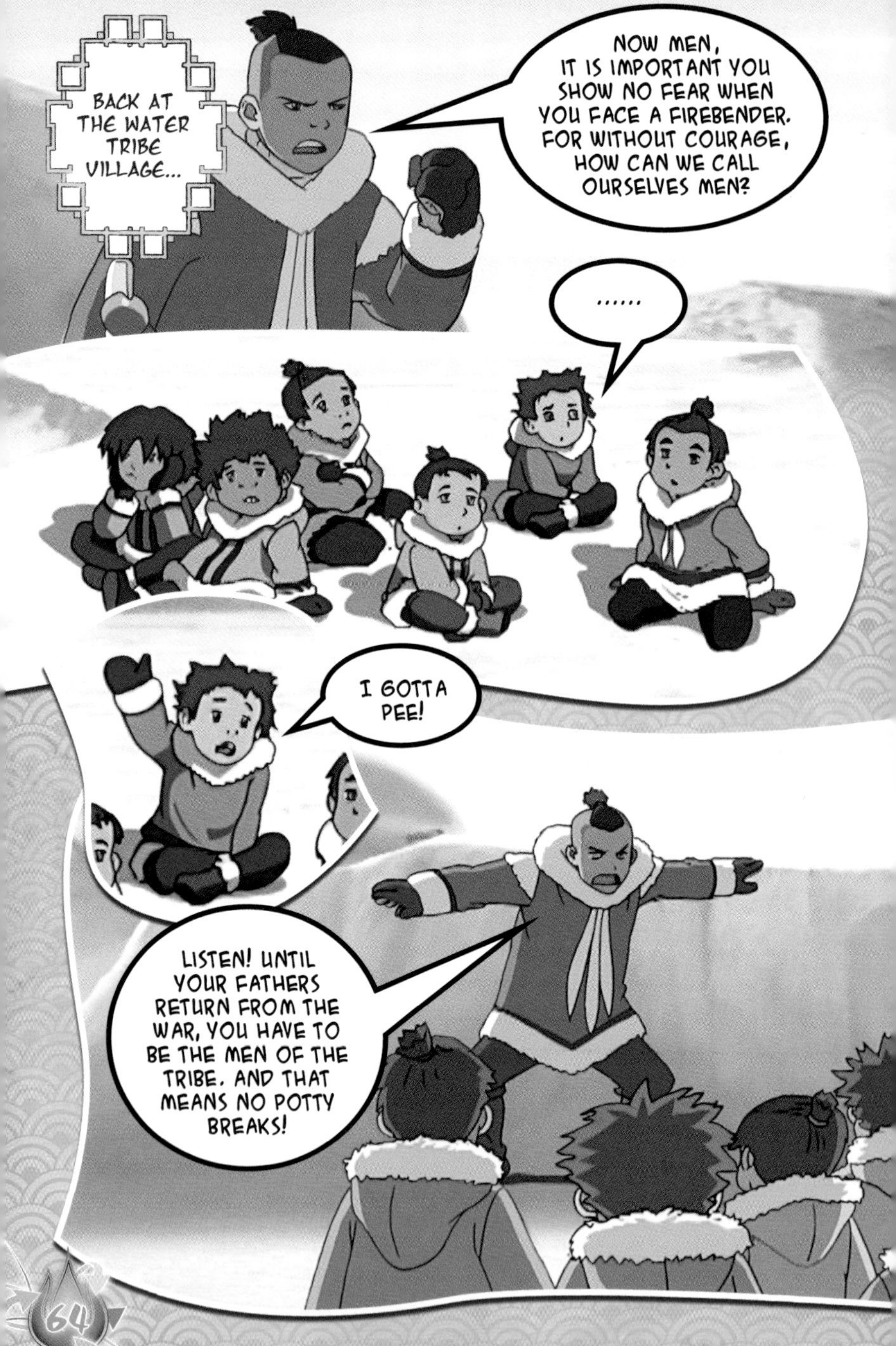
BACK AT THE WATER TRIBE VILLAGE...
NOW MEN, IT IS IMPORTANT YOU SHOW NO FEAR WHEN YOU FACE A FIREBENDER. FOR WITHOUT COURAGE, HOW CAN WE CALL OURSELVES MEN?
......
I GOTTA PEE!
LISTEN! UNTIL YOUR FATHERS RETURN FROM THE WAR, YOU HAVE TO BE THE MEN OF THE TRIBE. AND THAT MEANS NO POTTY BREAKS!

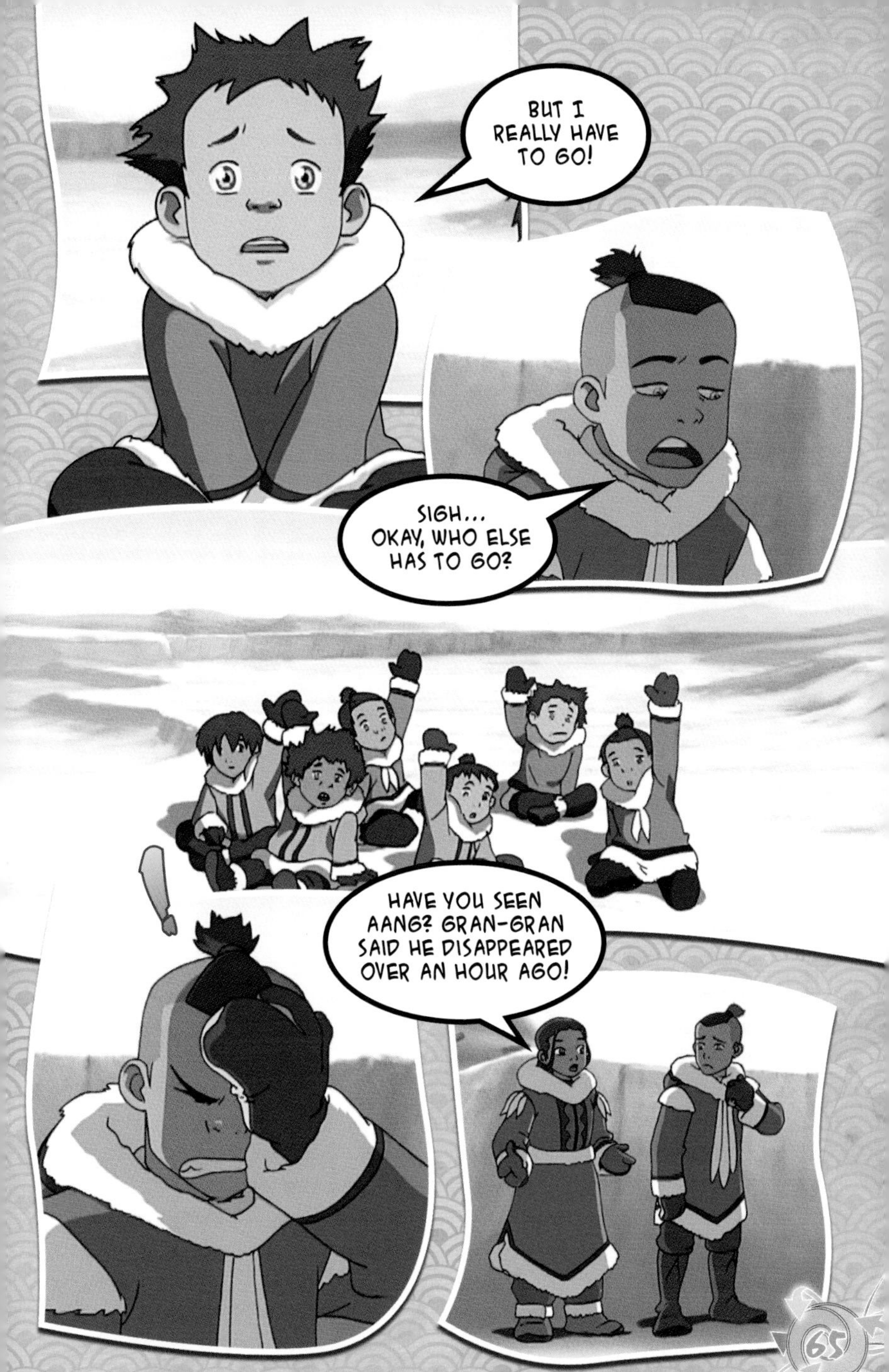
BUT I REALLY HAVE TO GO!
SIGH... OKAY, WHO ELSE HAS TO GO?
HAVE YOU SEEN AANG? GRAN-GRAN SAID HE DISAPPEARED OVER AN HOUR AGO!

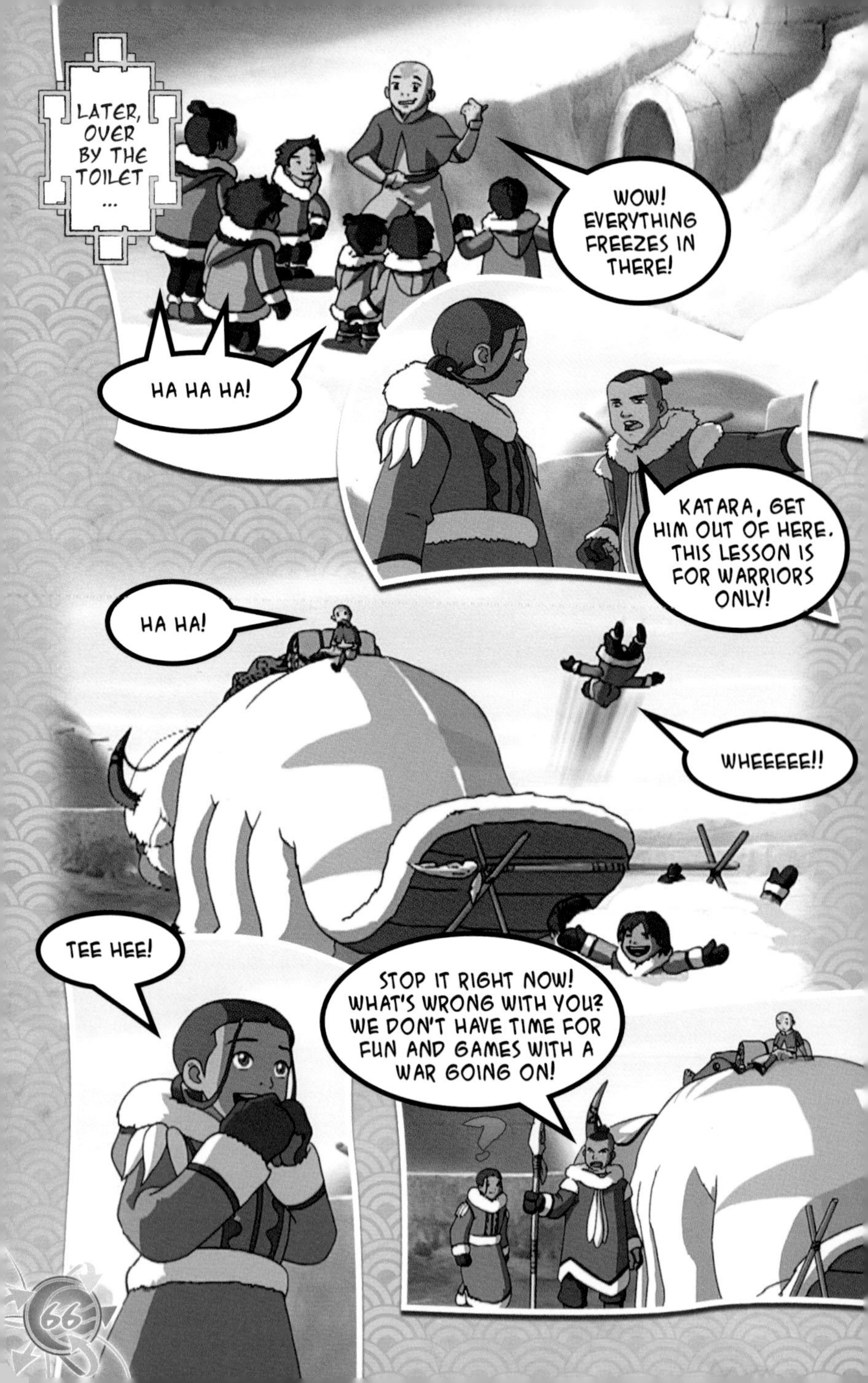
LATER, OVER BY THE TOILET ...
WOW! EVERYTHING FREEZES IN THERE!
HA HA HA!
KATARA, GET HIM OUT OF HERE. THIS LESSON IS FOR WARRIORS ONLY!
HA HA!
WHEEEEE!!
TEE HEE!
STOP IT RIGHT NOW! WHAT'S WRONG WITH YOU? WE DON'T HAVE TIME FOR FUN AND GAMES WITH A WAR GOING ON!
66

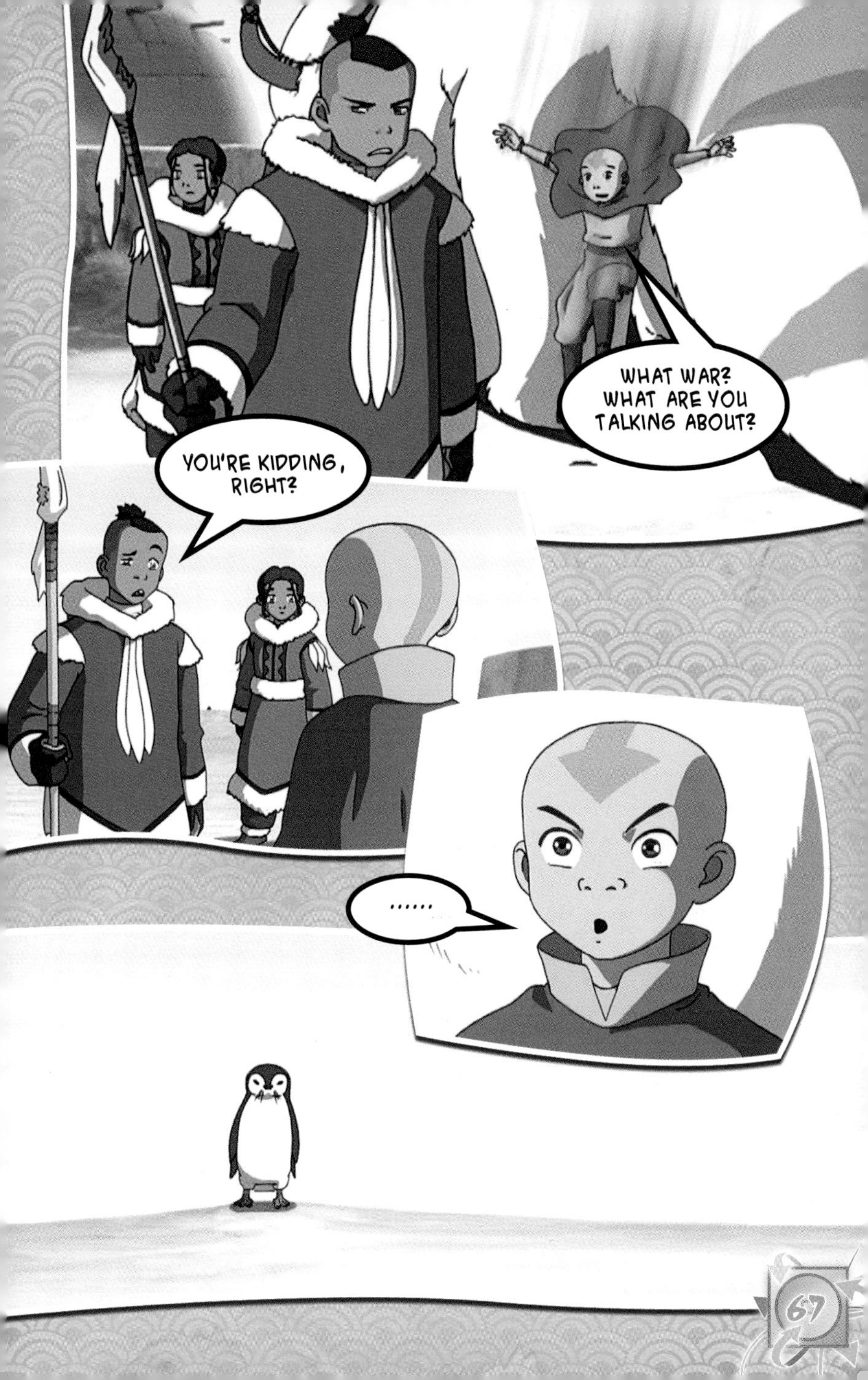
WHAT WAR? WHAT ARE YOU TALKING ABOUT?
YOU'RE KIDDING, RIGHT?
......

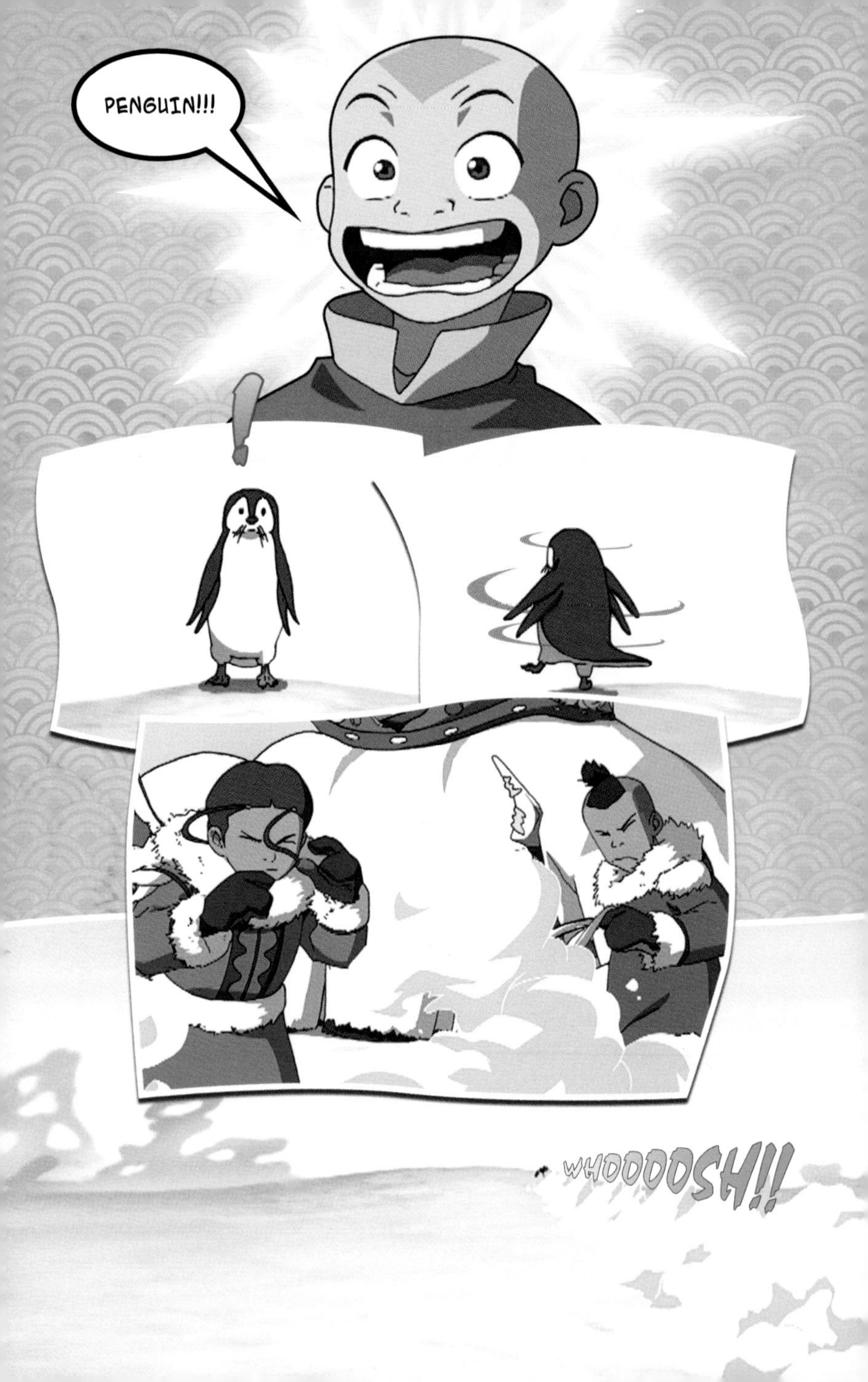
PENGUIN!!!
WHOOOOOSH!!

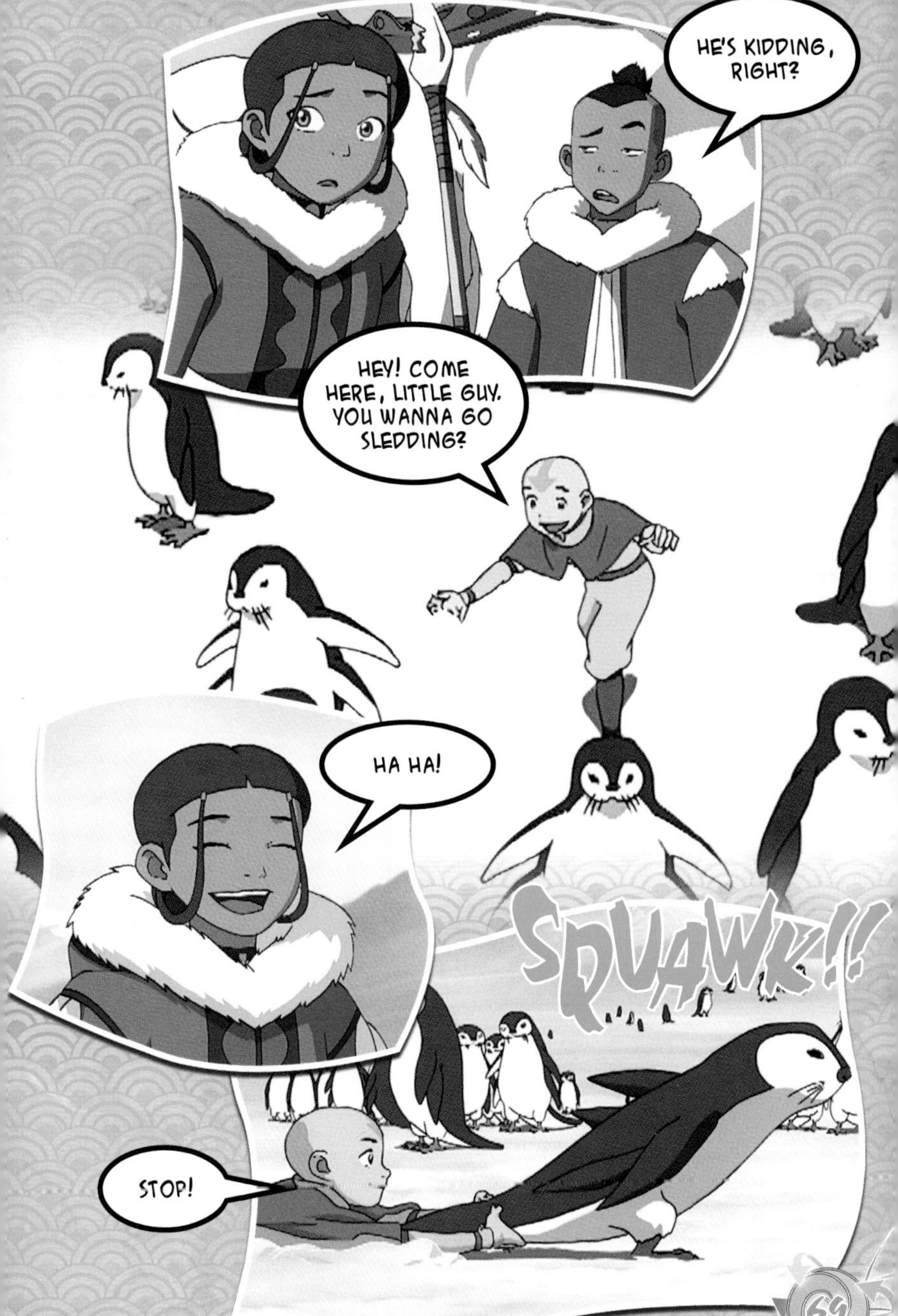
HE'S KIDDING, RIGHT?
HEY! COME HERE, LITTLE GUY. YOU WANNA GO SLEDDING?
HA HA!
SQUAWK!!
STOP!

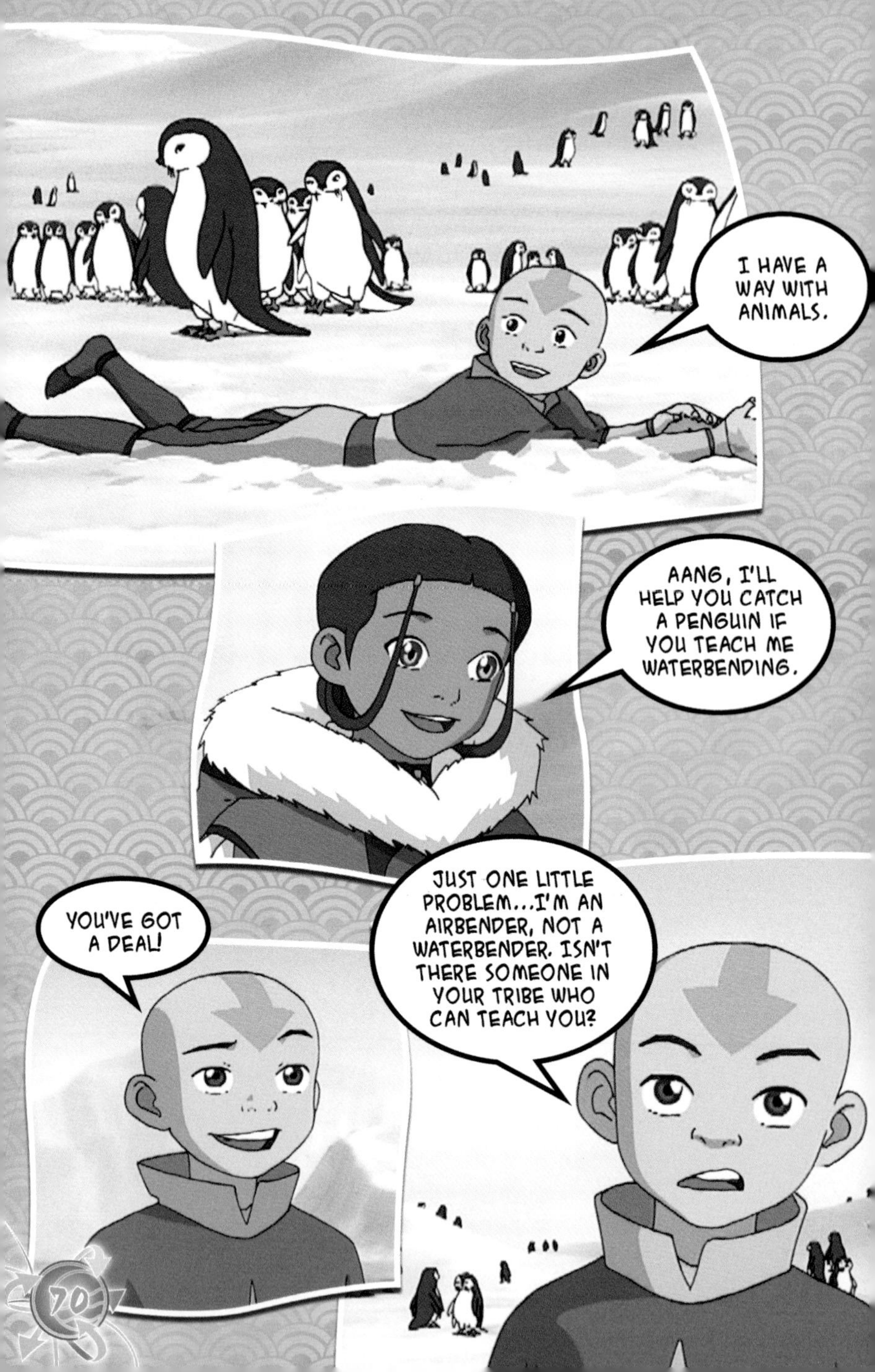
I HAVE A WAY WITH ANIMALS.
AANG, I'LL HELP YOU CATCH A PENGUIN IF YOU TEACH ME WATERBENDING.
YOU'VE GOT A DEAL!
JUST ONE LITTLE PROBLEM...I'M AN AIRBENDER, NOT A WATERBENDER. ISN'T THERE SOMEONE IN YOUR TRIBE WHO CAN TEACH YOU?

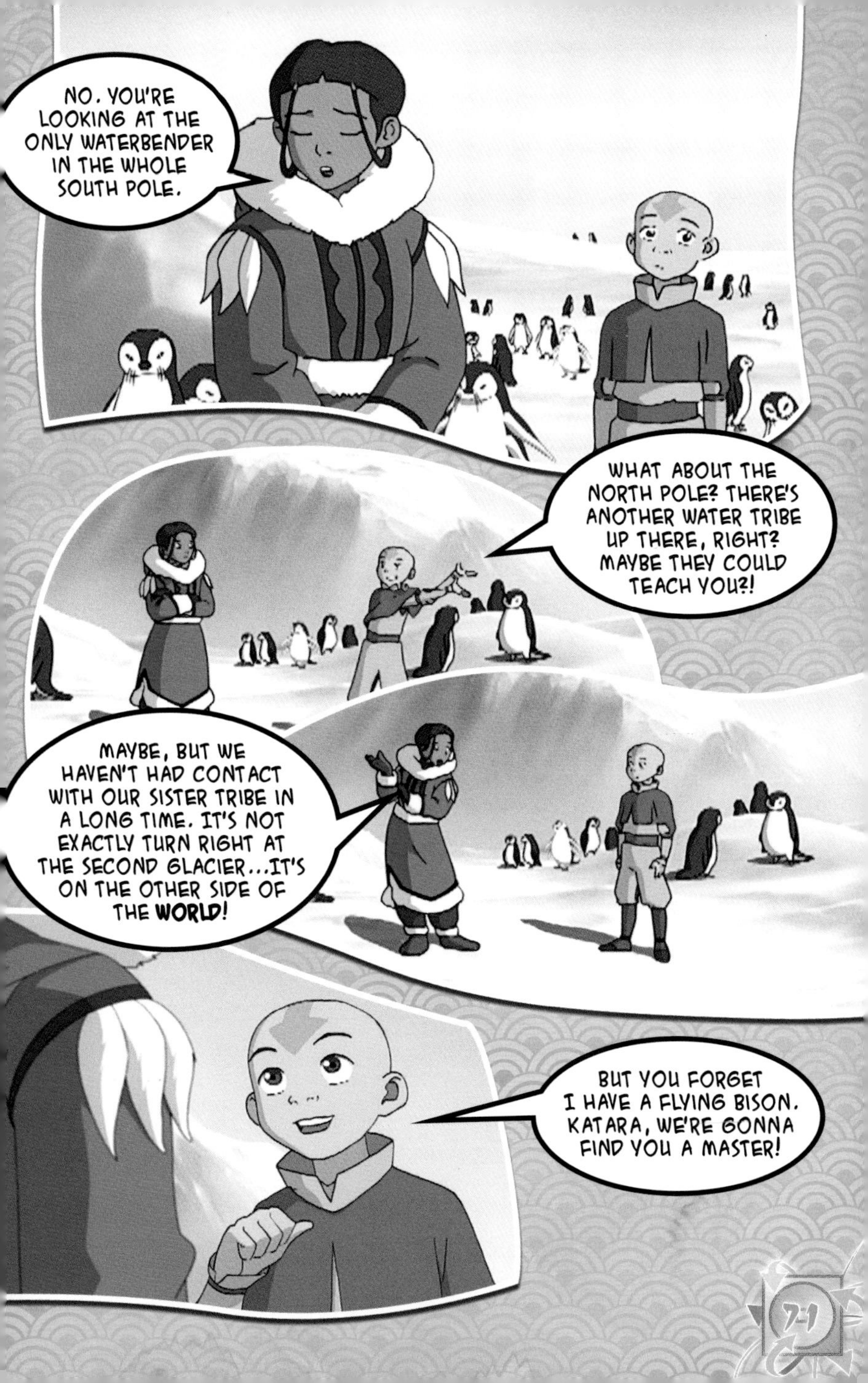

NO. YOU'RE LOOKING AT THE ONLY WATERBENDER IN THE WHOLE SOUTH POLE.
WHAT ABOUT THE NORTH POLE? THERE'S ANOTHER WATER TRIBE UP THERE, RIGHT? MAYBE THEY COULD TEACH YOU?!
MAYBE, BUT WE HAVEN'T HAD CONTACT WITH OUR SISTER TRIBE IN A LONG TIME. IT'S NOT EXACTLY TURN RIGHT AT THE SECOND GLACIER...IT'S ON THE OTHER SIDE OF THE **WORLD**!
BUT YOU FORGET I HAVE A FLYING BISON. KATARA, WE'RE GONNA FIND YOU A MASTER!

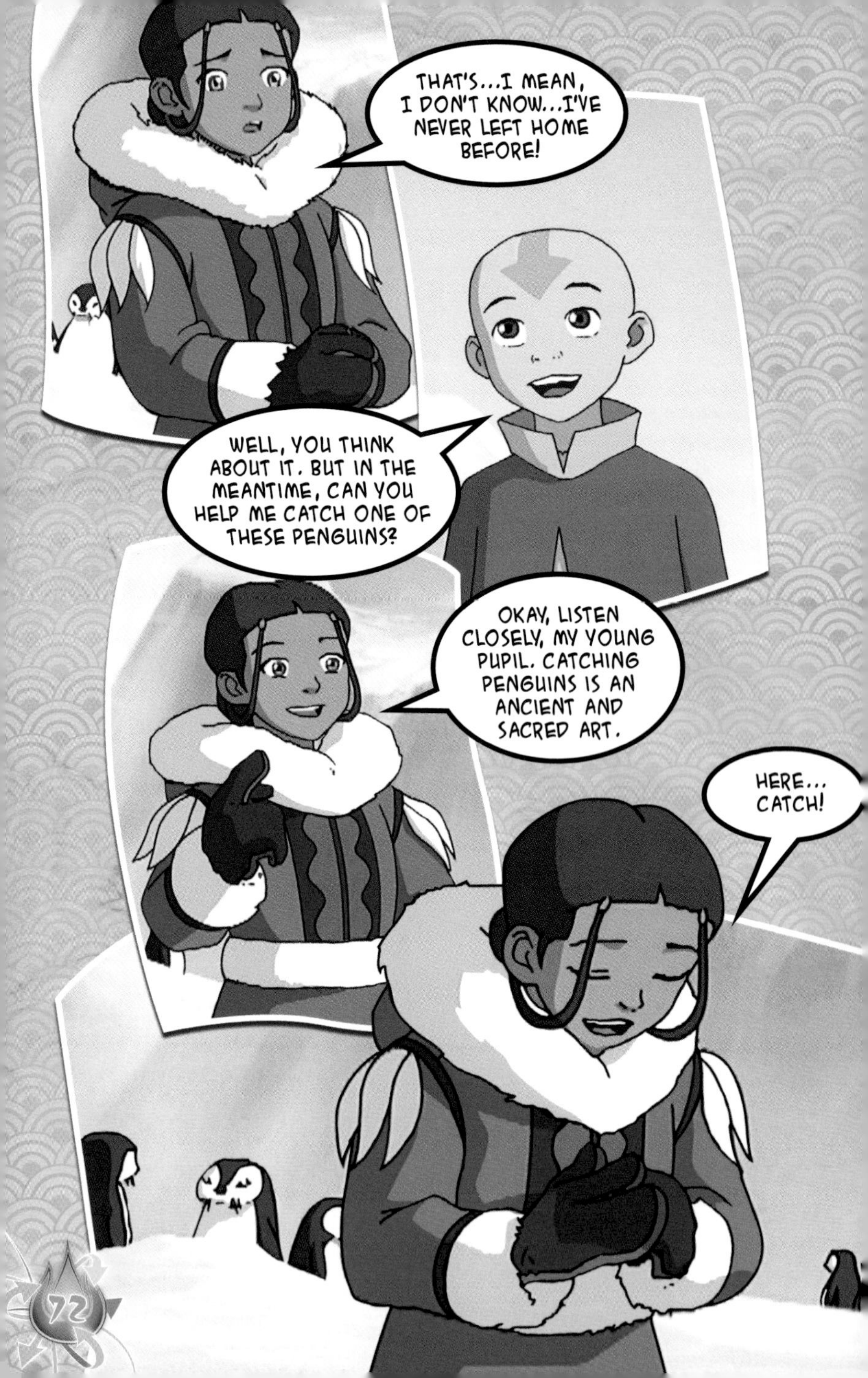
THAT'S...I MEAN, I DON'T KNOW...I'VE NEVER LEFT HOME BEFORE!
WELL, YOU THINK ABOUT IT. BUT IN THE MEANTIME, CAN YOU HELP ME CATCH ONE OF THESE PENGUINS?
OKAY, LISTEN CLOSELY, MY YOUNG PUPIL. CATCHING PENGUINS IS AN ANCIENT AND SACRED ART.
HERE... CATCH!

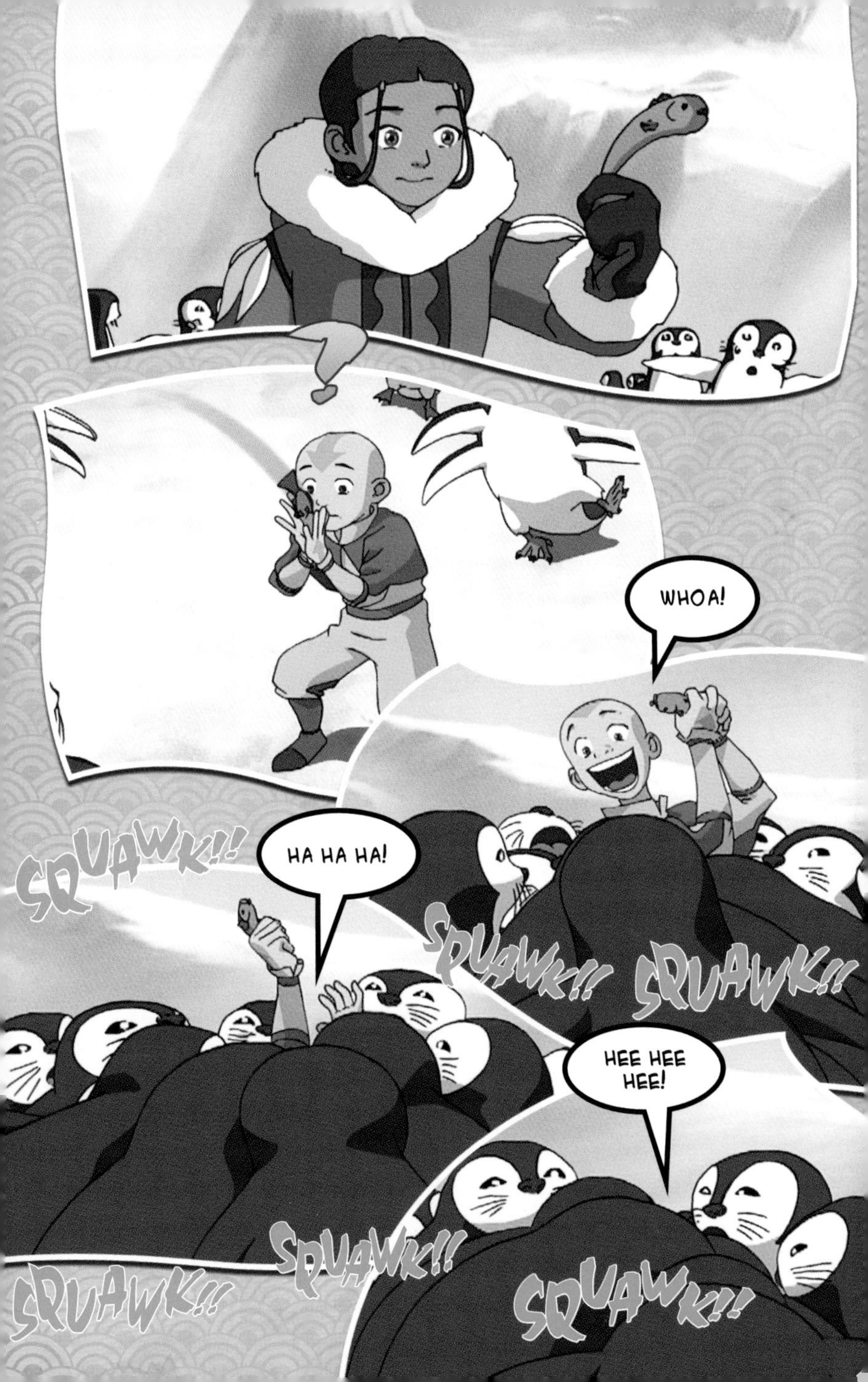
WHOA!
SQUAWK!!
HA HA HA!
SQUAWK!!
SQUAWK!!
HEE HEE HEE!
SQUAWK!!
SQUAWK!!
SQUAWK!!

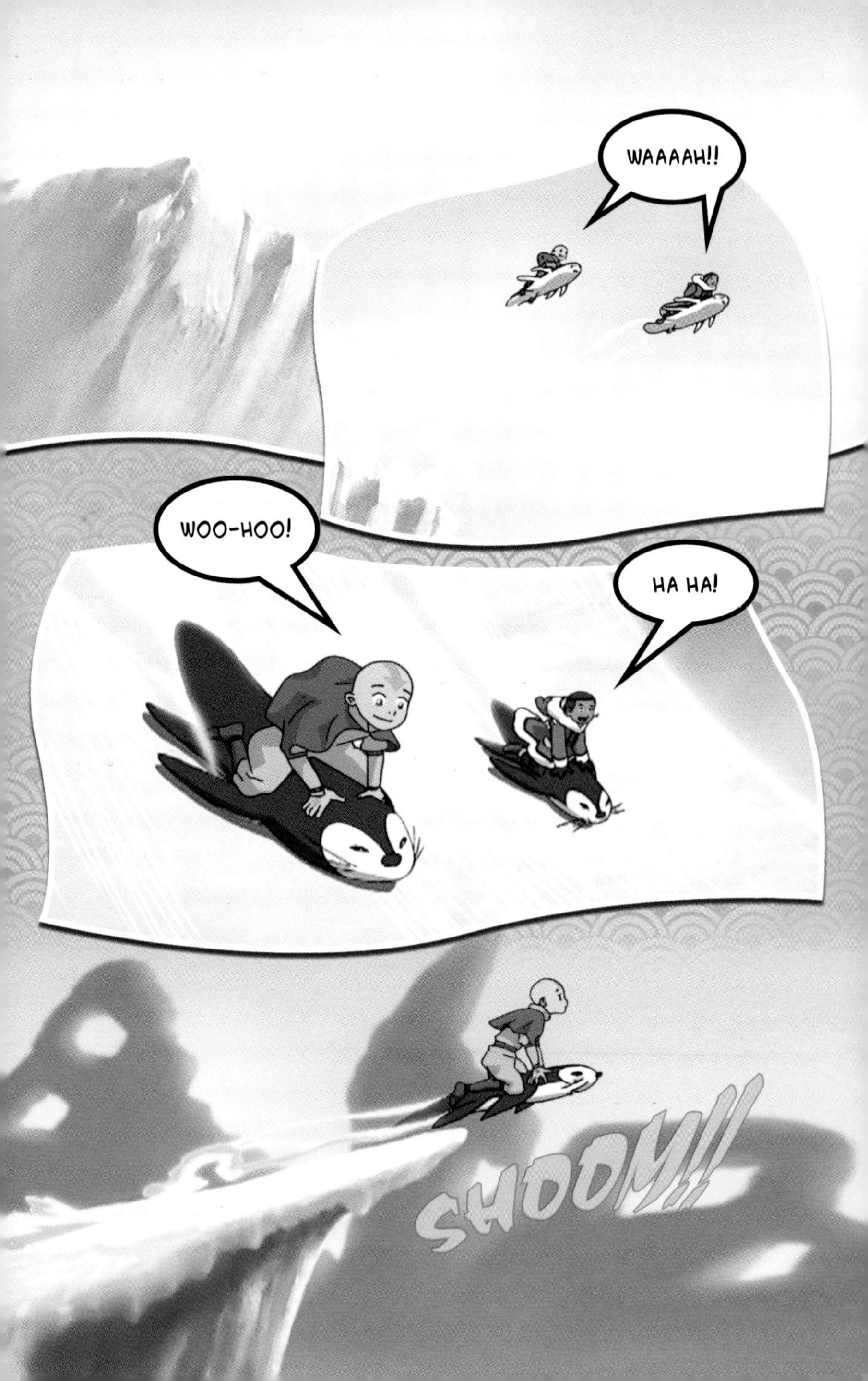
WAAAAH!!
WOO-HOO!
HA HA!
SHOOM!!

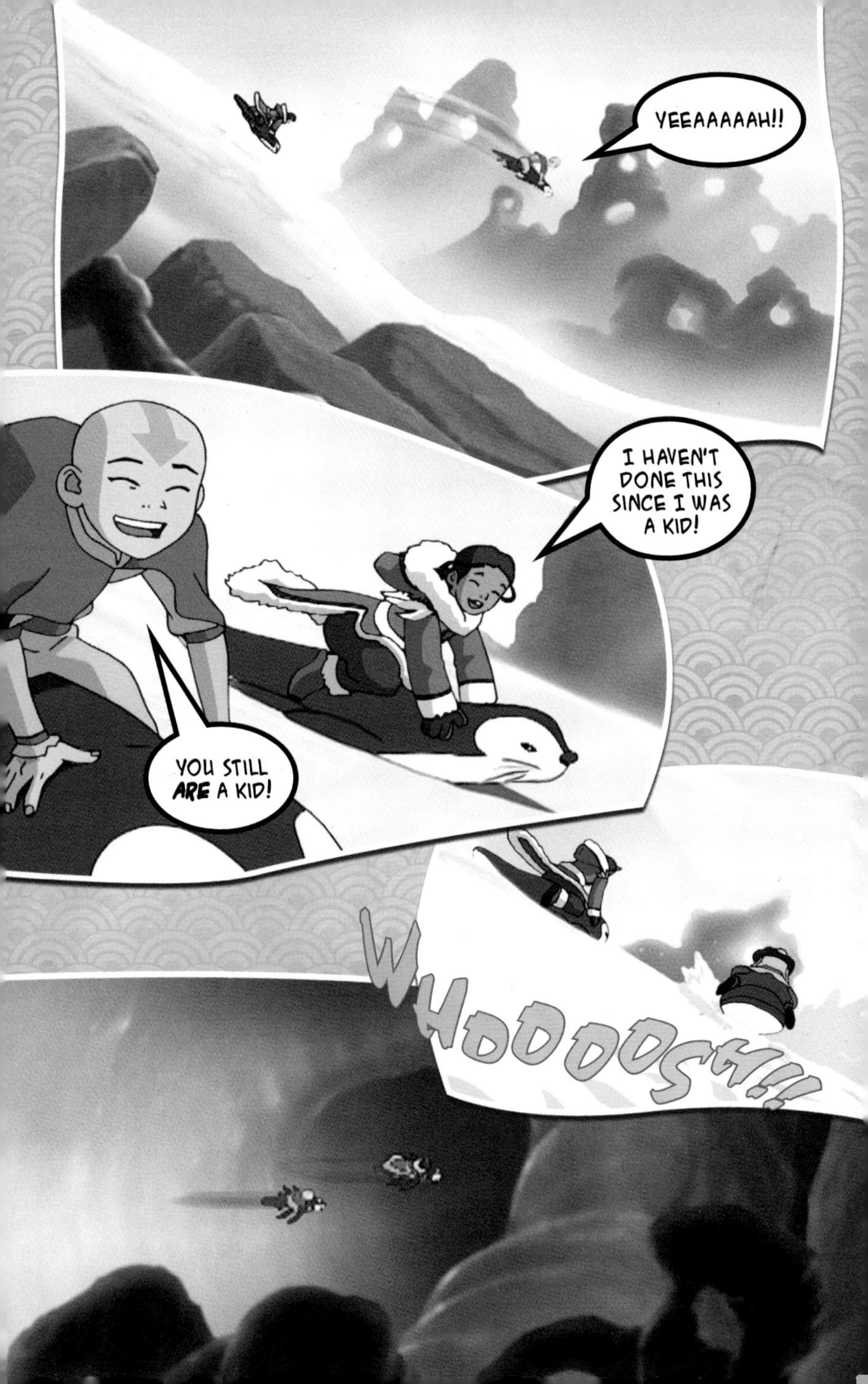
YEEAAAAAH!!
I HAVEN'T DONE THIS SINCE I WAS A KID!
YOU STILL **ARE** A KID!
WHOOOOSH!!

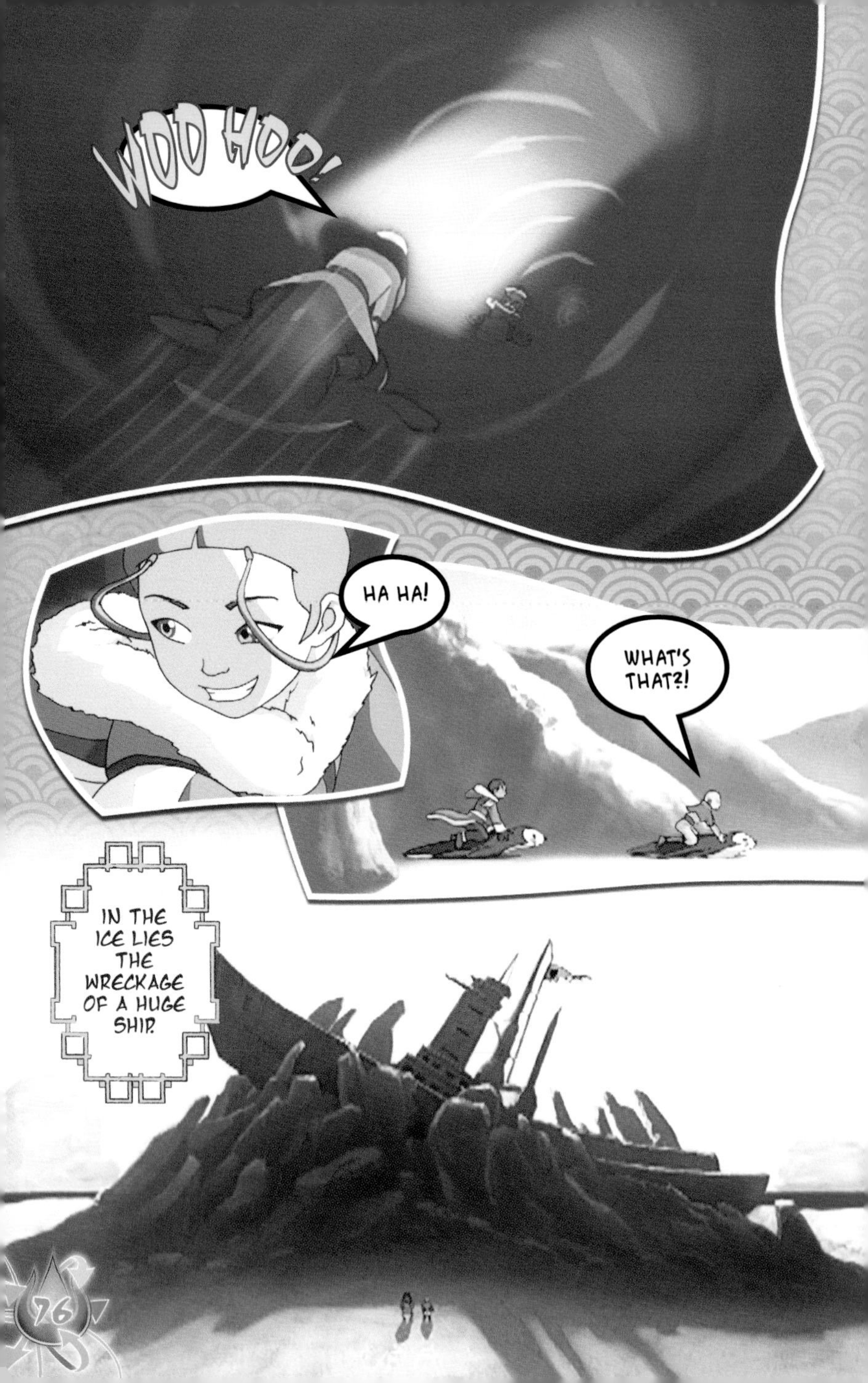
WOO HOO!
HA HA!
WHAT'S THAT?!
IN THE ICE LIES THE WRECKAGE OF A HUGE SHIP.

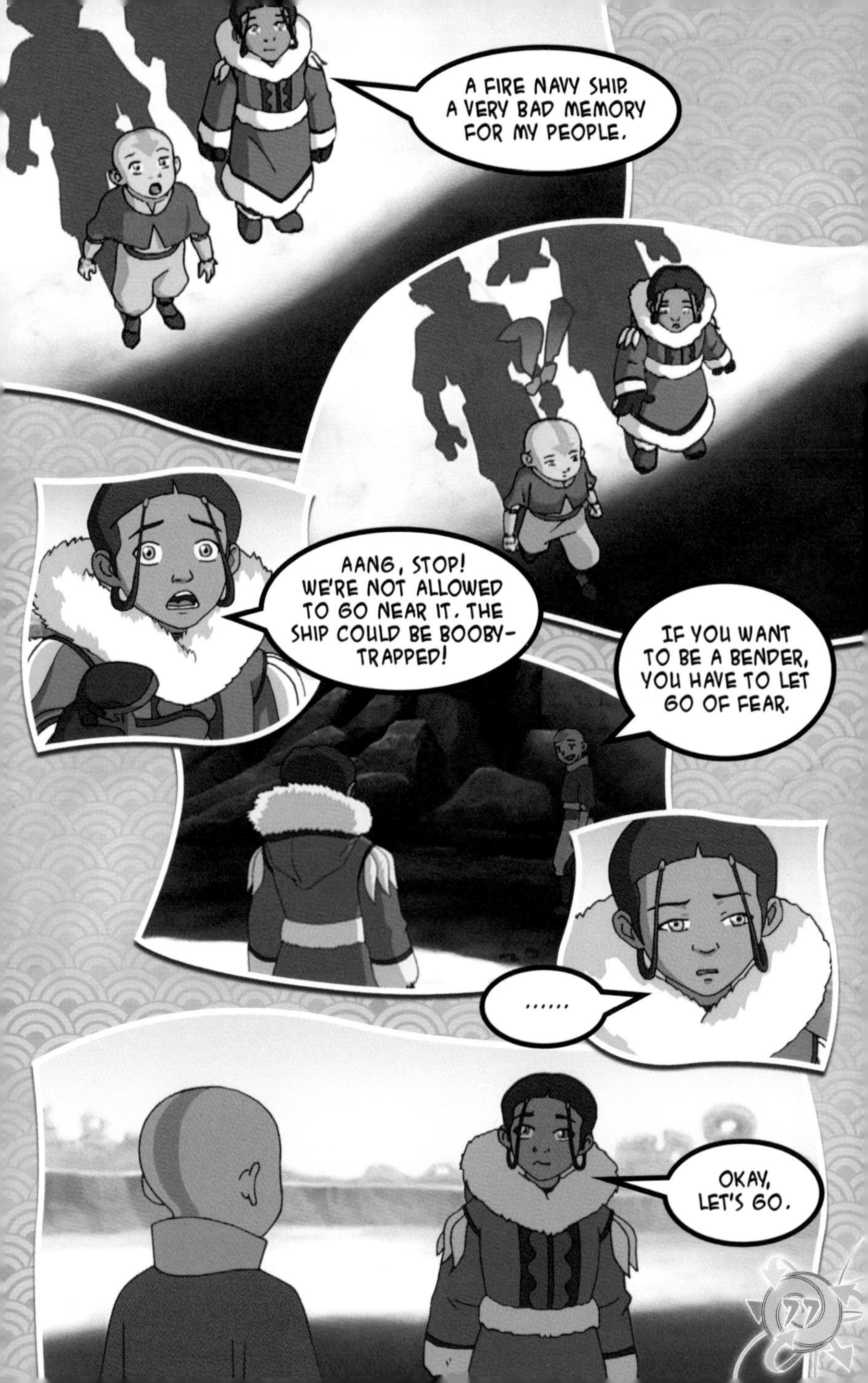
A FIRE NAVY SHIP. A VERY BAD MEMORY FOR MY PEOPLE.
AANG, STOP! WE'RE NOT ALLOWED TO GO NEAR IT. THE SHIP COULD BE BOOBY-TRAPPED!
IF YOU WANT TO BE A BENDER, YOU HAVE TO LET GO OF FEAR.
......
OKAY, LET'S GO.

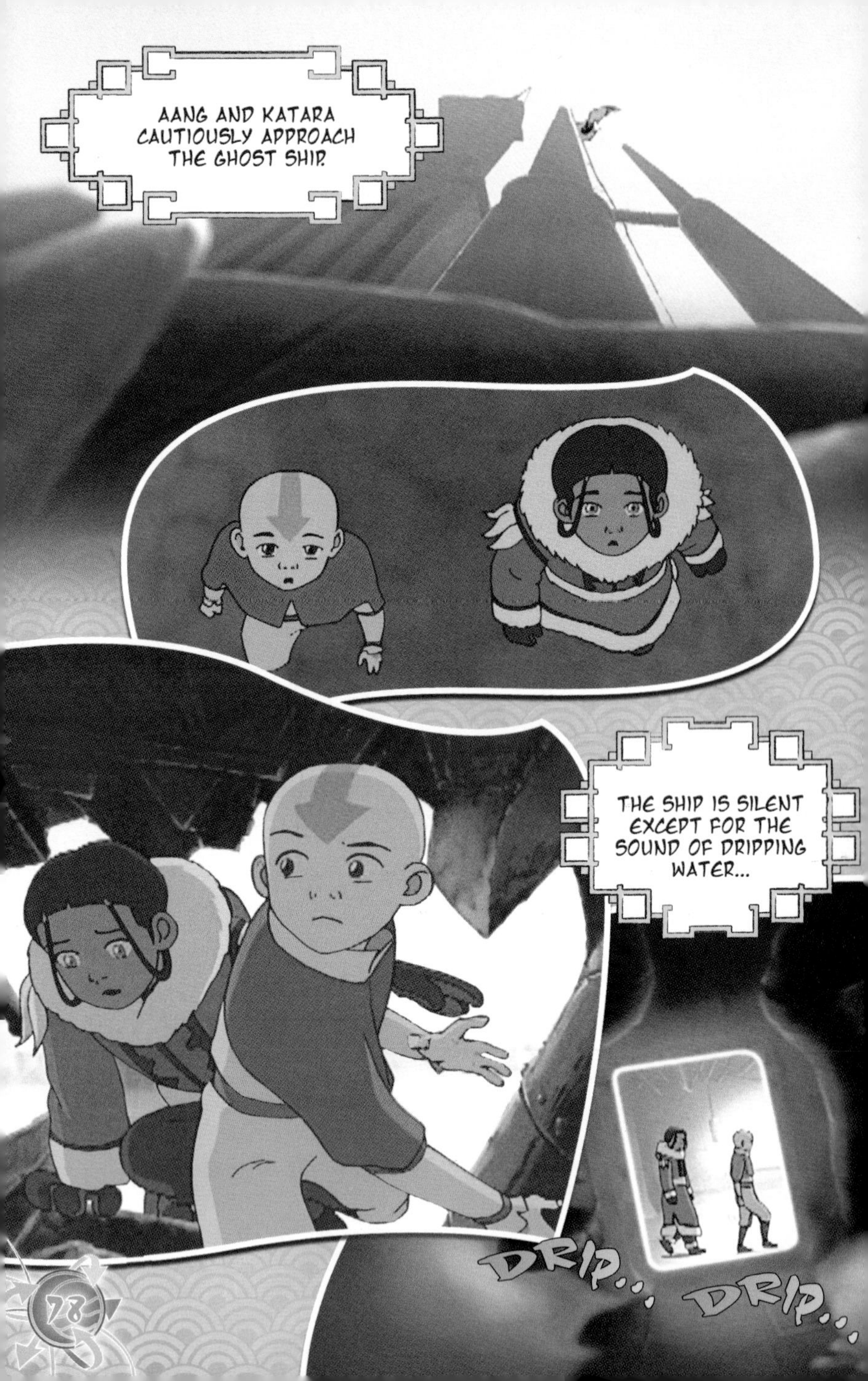
AANG AND KATARA CAUTIOUSLY APPROACH THE GHOST SHIP.
THE SHIP IS SILENT EXCEPT FOR THE SOUND OF DRIPPING WATER...
DRIP... DRIP...

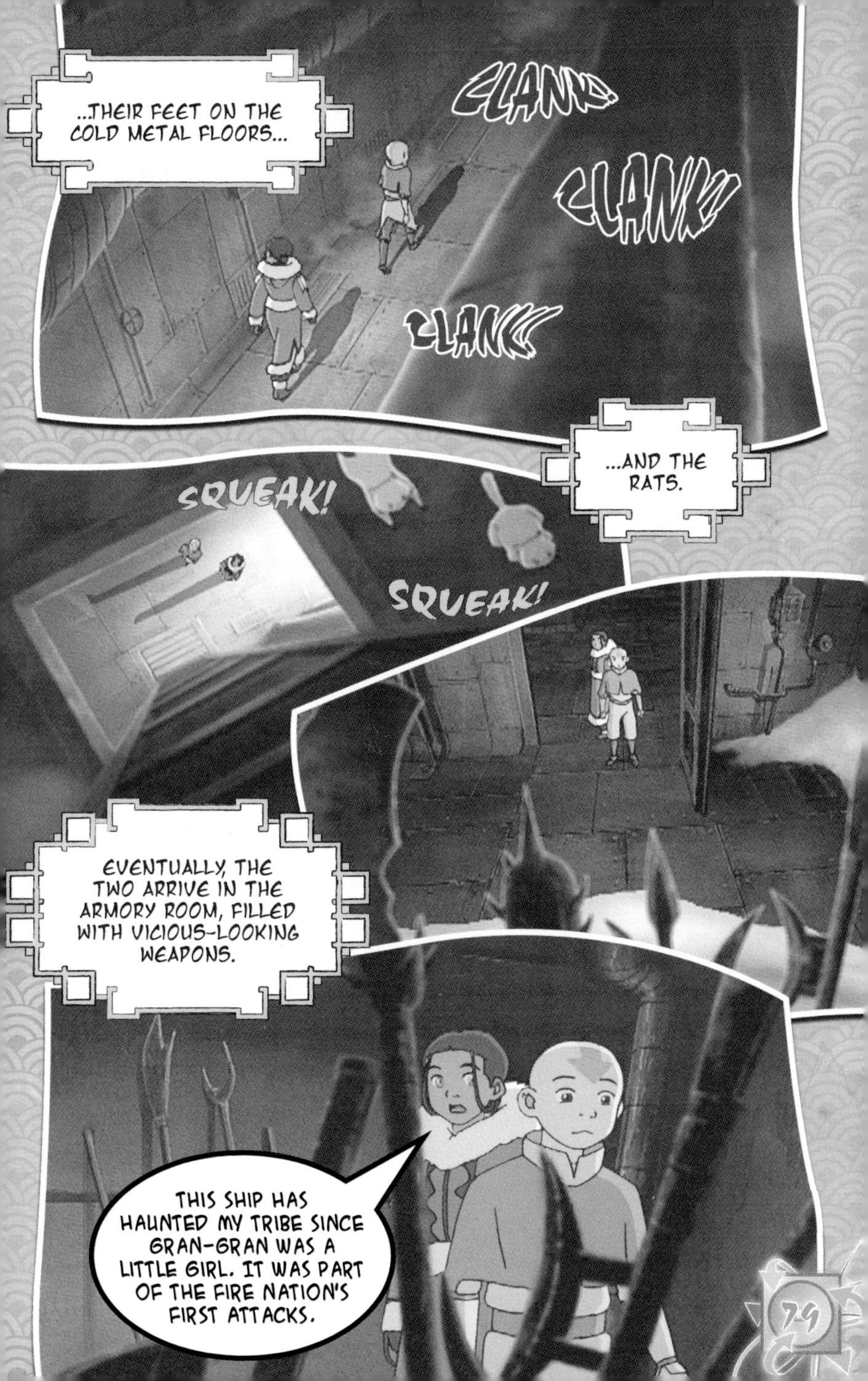
...THEIR FEET ON THE COLD METAL FLOORS...
CLANK!
CLANK!
CLANK!
...AND THE RATS.
SQUEAK!
SQUEAK!
EVENTUALLY, THE TWO ARRIVE IN THE ARMORY ROOM, FILLED WITH VICIOUS-LOOKING WEAPONS.
THIS SHIP HAS HAUNTED MY TRIBE SINCE GRAN-GRAN WAS A LITTLE GIRL. IT WAS PART OF THE FIRE NATION'S FIRST ATTACKS.

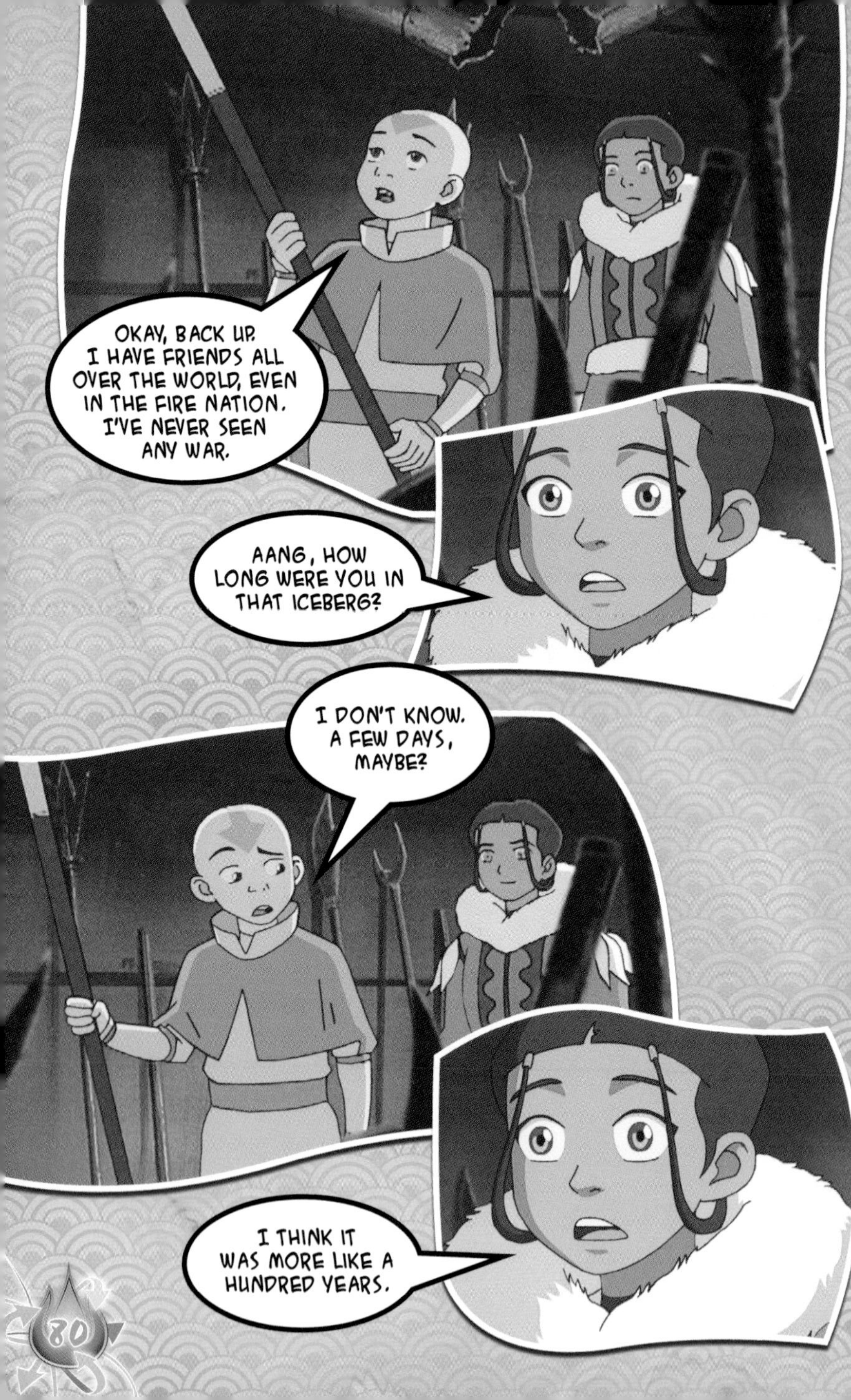
OKAY, BACK UP. I HAVE FRIENDS ALL OVER THE WORLD, EVEN IN THE FIRE NATION. I'VE NEVER SEEN ANY WAR.
AANG, HOW LONG WERE YOU IN THAT ICEBERG?
I DON'T KNOW. A FEW DAYS, MAYBE?
I THINK IT WAS MORE LIKE A HUNDRED YEARS.

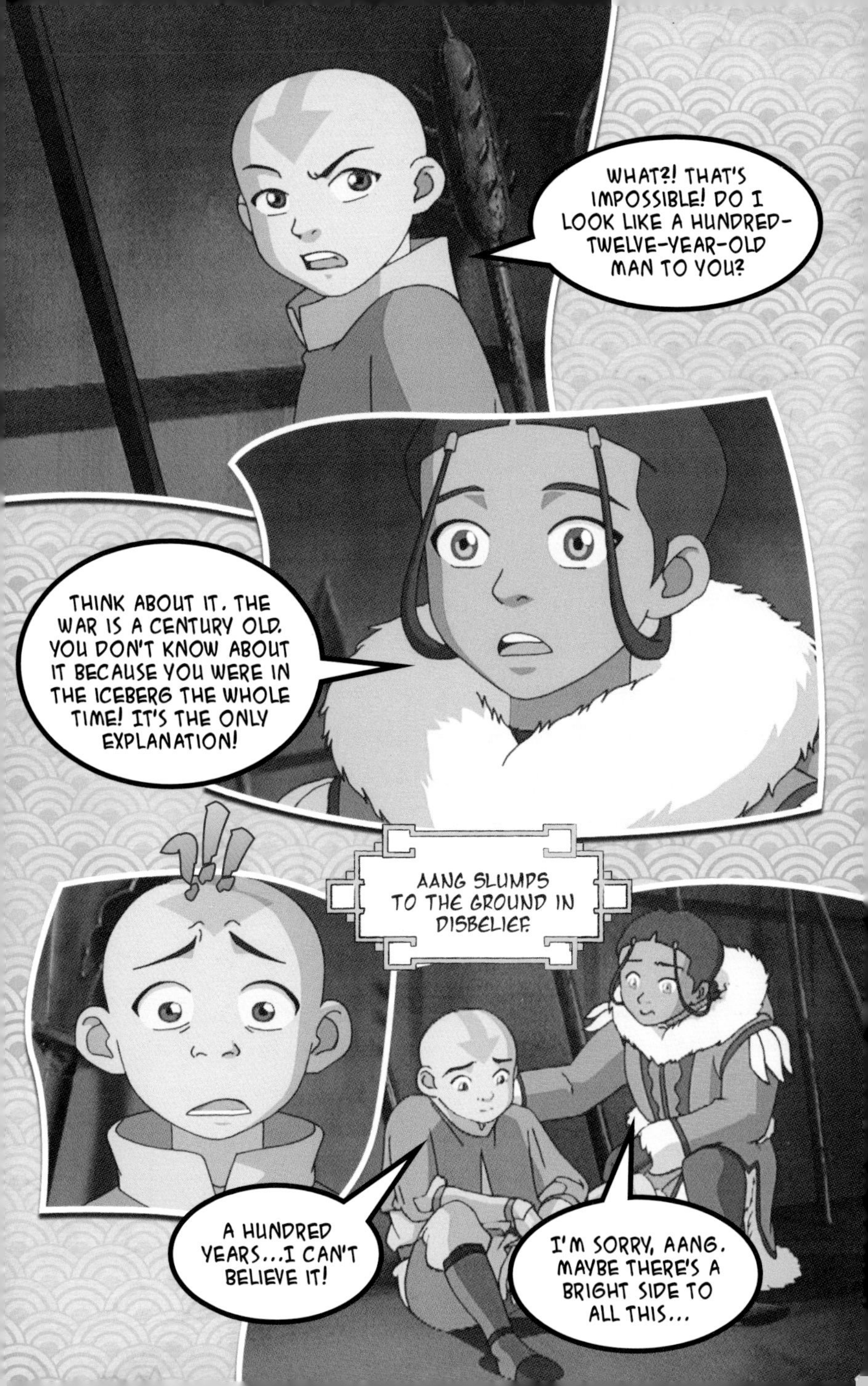
WHAT?! THAT'S IMPOSSIBLE! DO I LOOK LIKE A HUNDRED-TWELVE-YEAR-OLD MAN TO YOU?
THINK ABOUT IT. THE WAR IS A CENTURY OLD. YOU DON'T KNOW ABOUT IT BECAUSE YOU WERE IN THE ICEBERG THE WHOLE TIME! IT'S THE ONLY EXPLANATION!
AANG SLUMPS TO THE GROUND IN DISBELIEF.
A HUNDRED YEARS...I CAN'T BELIEVE IT!
I'M SORRY, AANG. MAYBE THERE'S A BRIGHT SIDE TO ALL THIS...

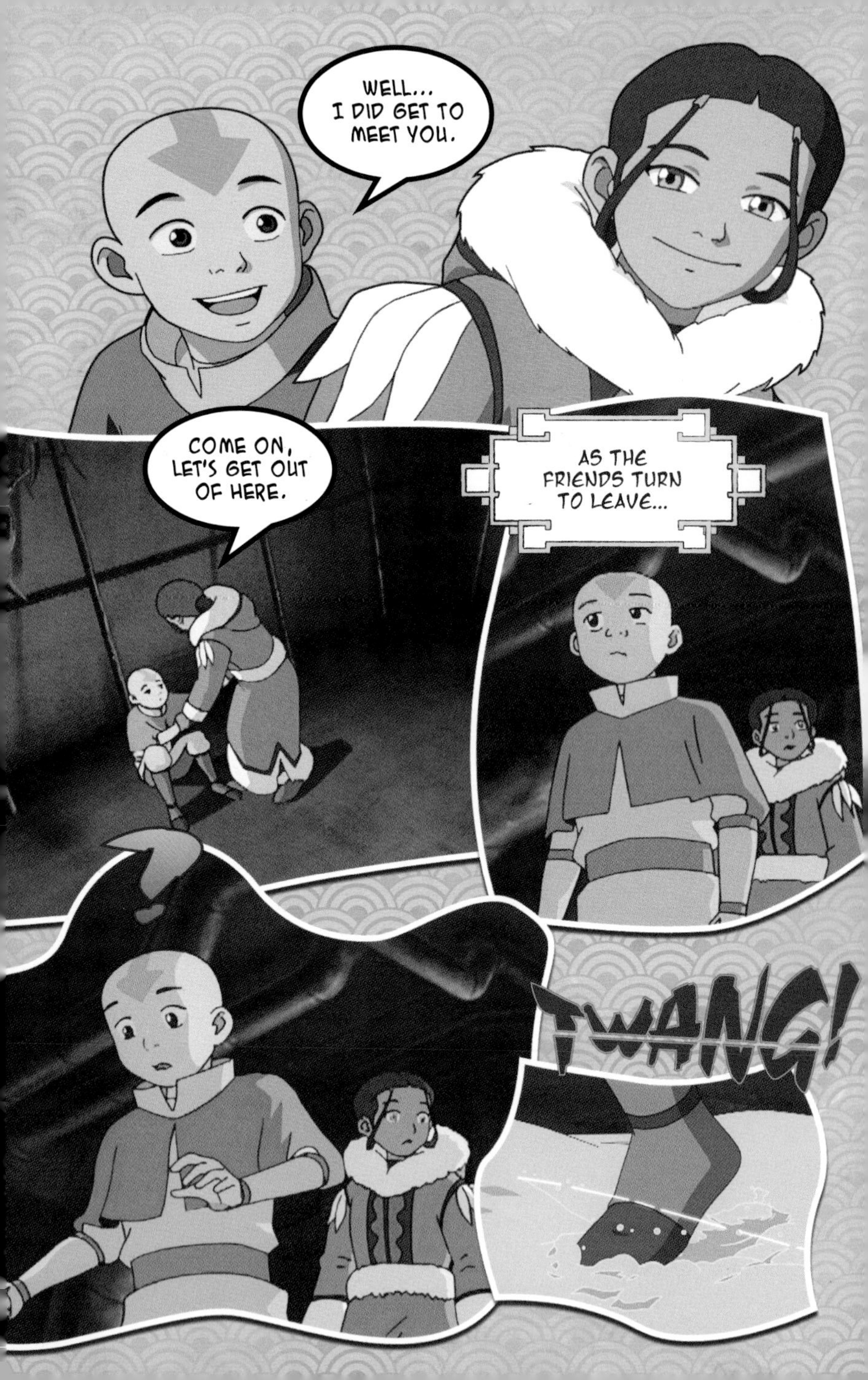
WELL... I DID GET TO MEET YOU.
COME ON, LET'S GET OUT OF HERE.
AS THE FRIENDS TURN TO LEAVE...
TWANG!

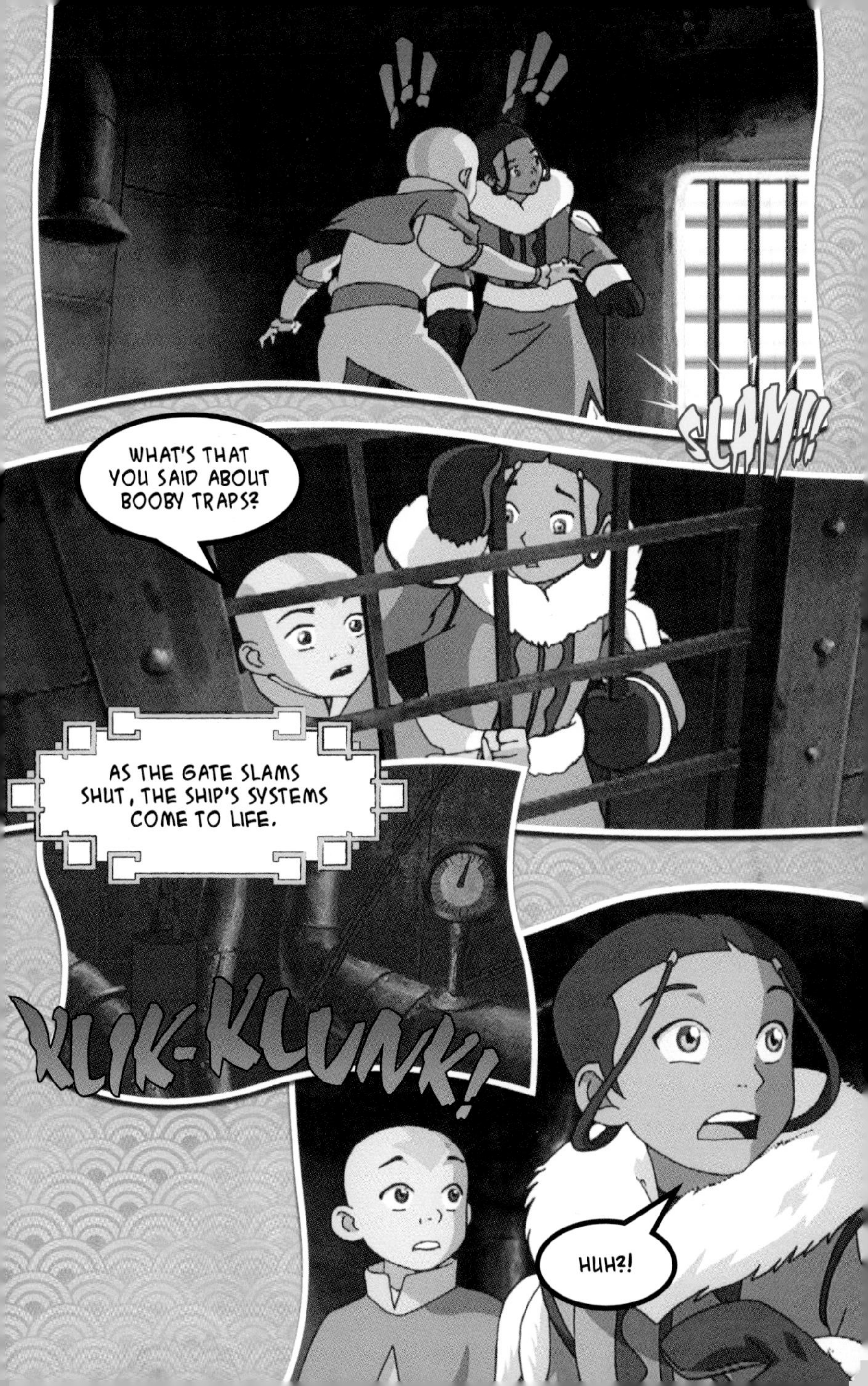
!!!
!!!
SLAM!!
WHAT'S THAT YOU SAID ABOUT BOOBY TRAPS?
AS THE GATE SLAMS SHUT, THE SHIP'S SYSTEMS COME TO LIFE.
KLIK-KLUNK!
HUH?!

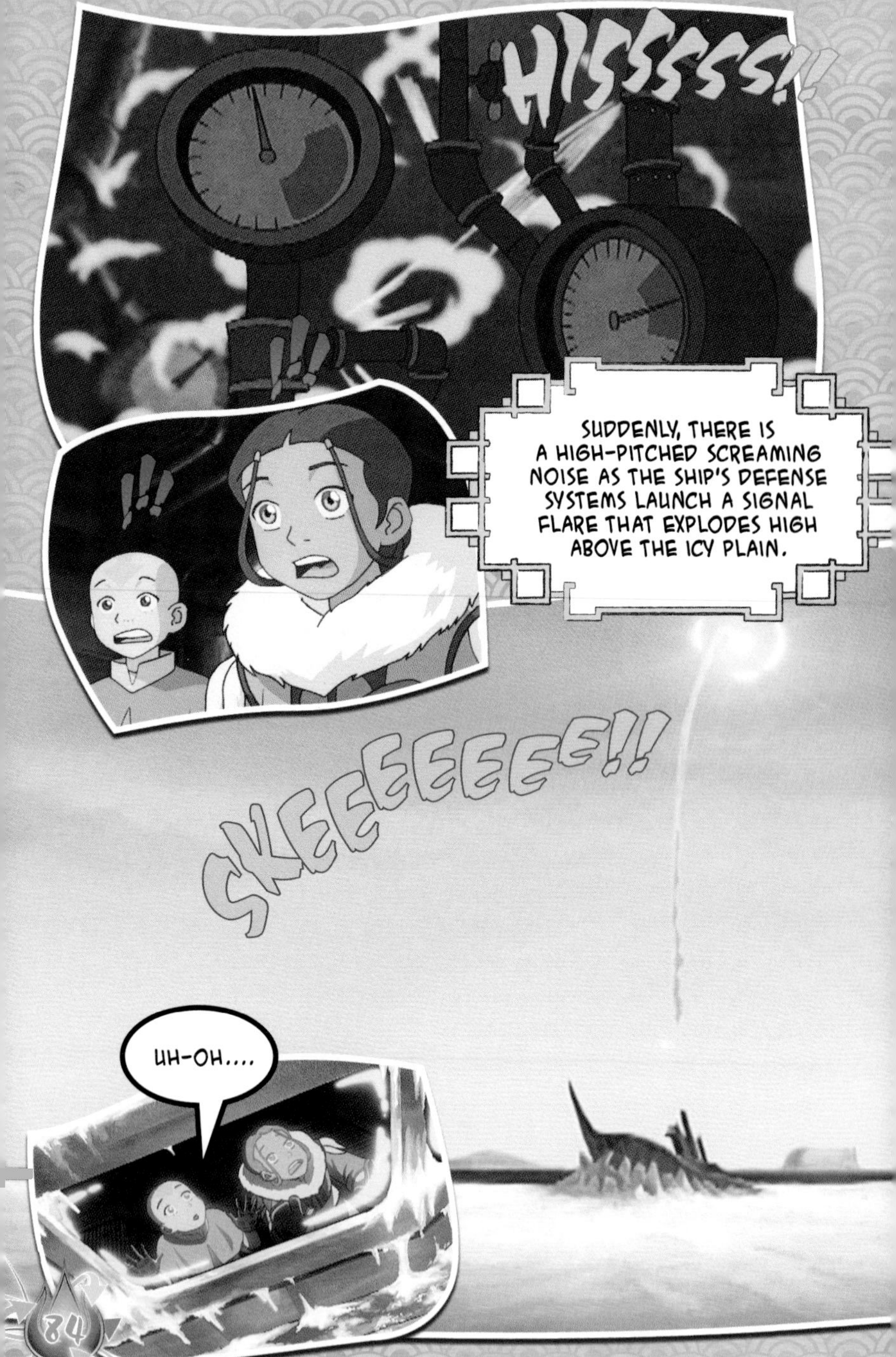
HISSSSS!!
!!!
!!!
SUDDENLY, THERE IS A HIGH-PITCHED SCREAMING NOISE AS THE SHIP'S DEFENSE SYSTEMS LAUNCH A SIGNAL FLARE THAT EXPLODES HIGH ABOVE THE ICY PLAIN.
SKEEEEEEE!!
UH-OH....

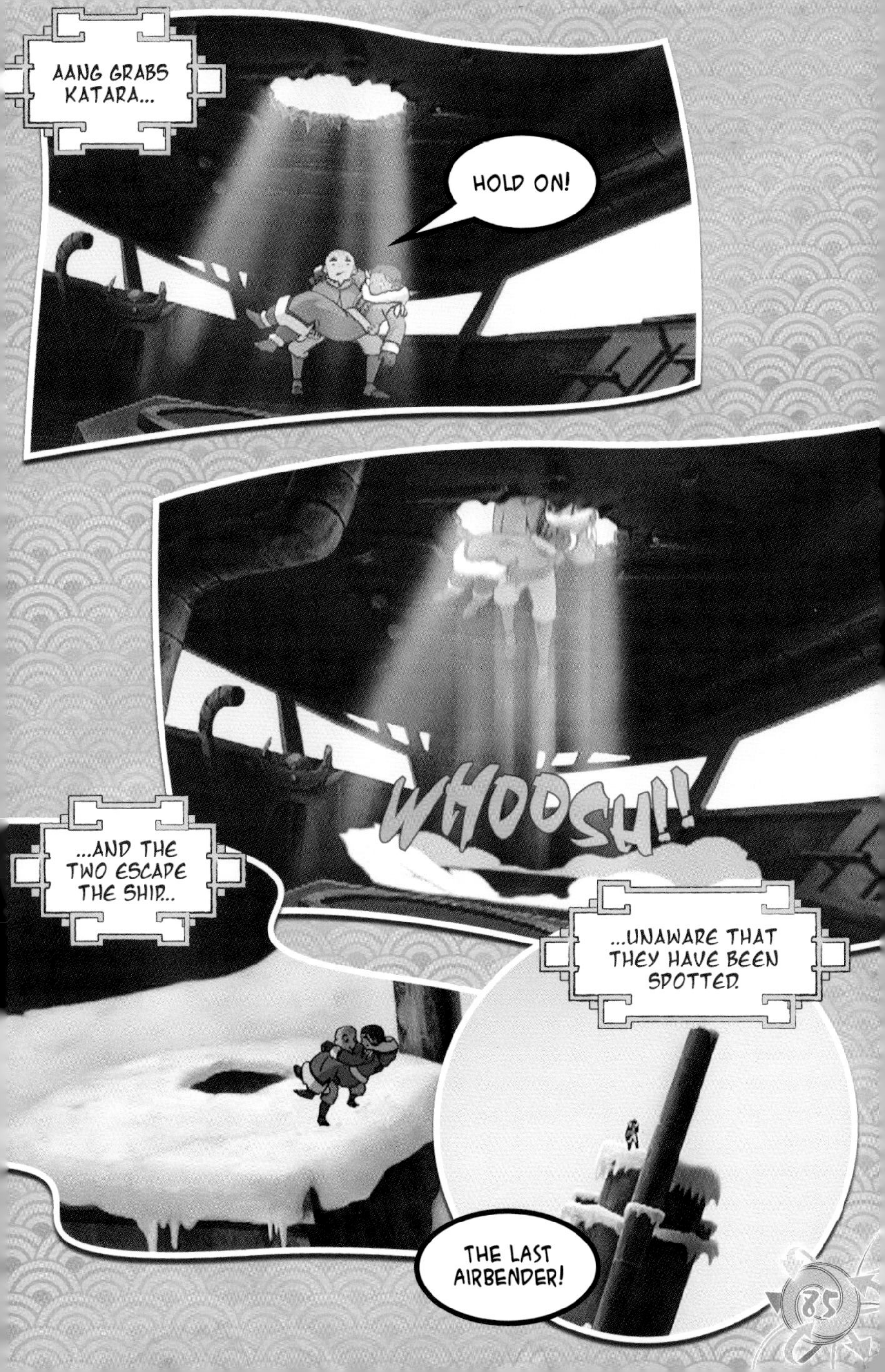
AANG GRABS KATARA...
HOLD ON!
WHOOSH!
...AND THE TWO ESCAPE THE SHIP...
...UNAWARE THAT THEY HAVE BEEN SPOTTED.
THE LAST AIRBENDER!

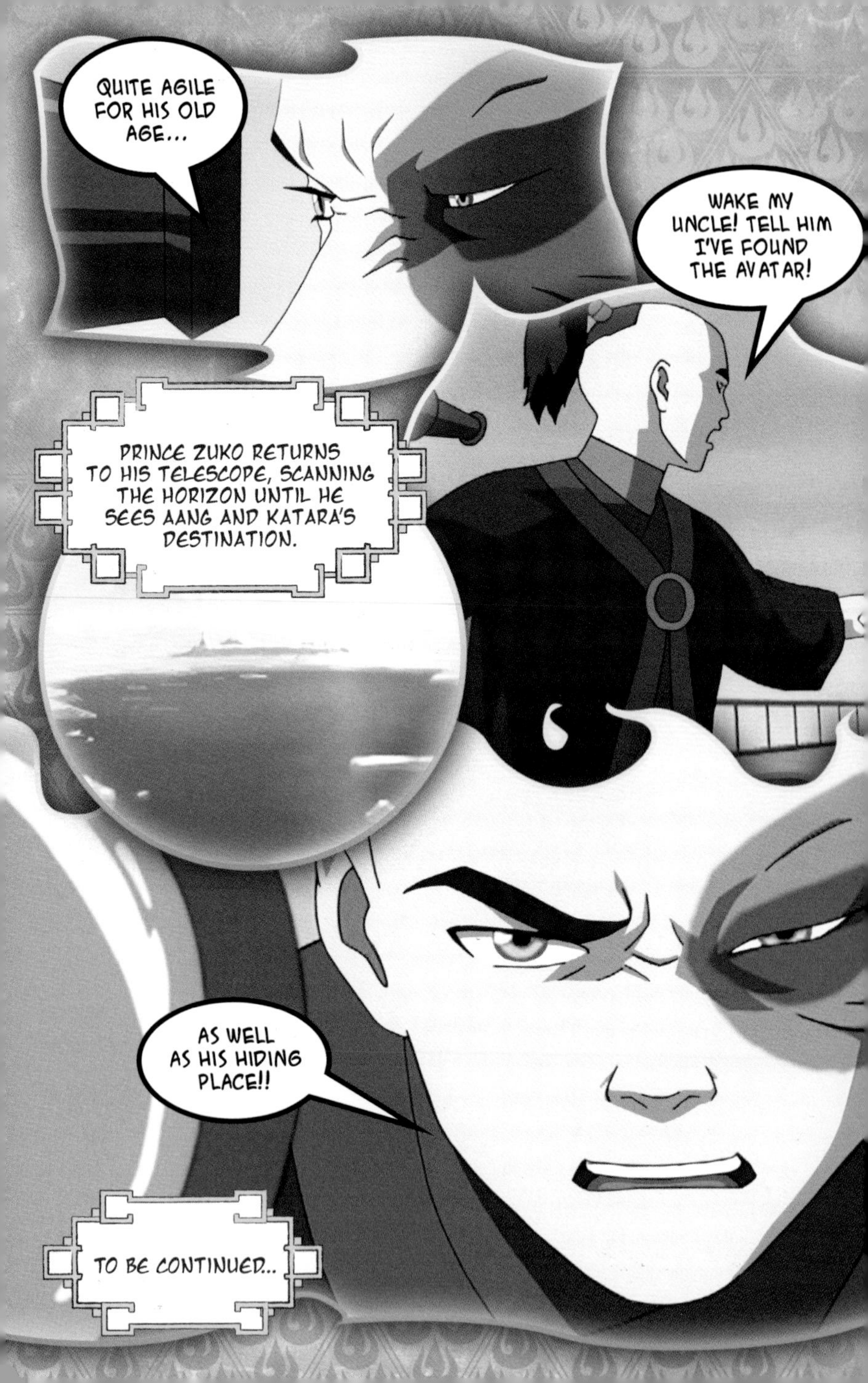
QUITE AGILE FOR HIS OLD AGE...
WAKE MY UNCLE! TELL HIM I'VE FOUND THE AVATAR!
PRINCE ZUKO RETURNS TO HIS TELESCOPE, SCANNING THE HORIZON UNTIL HE SEES AANG AND KATARA'S DESTINATION.
AS WELL AS HIS HIDING PLACE!!
TO BE CONTINUED...

THE FOUR NATIONS

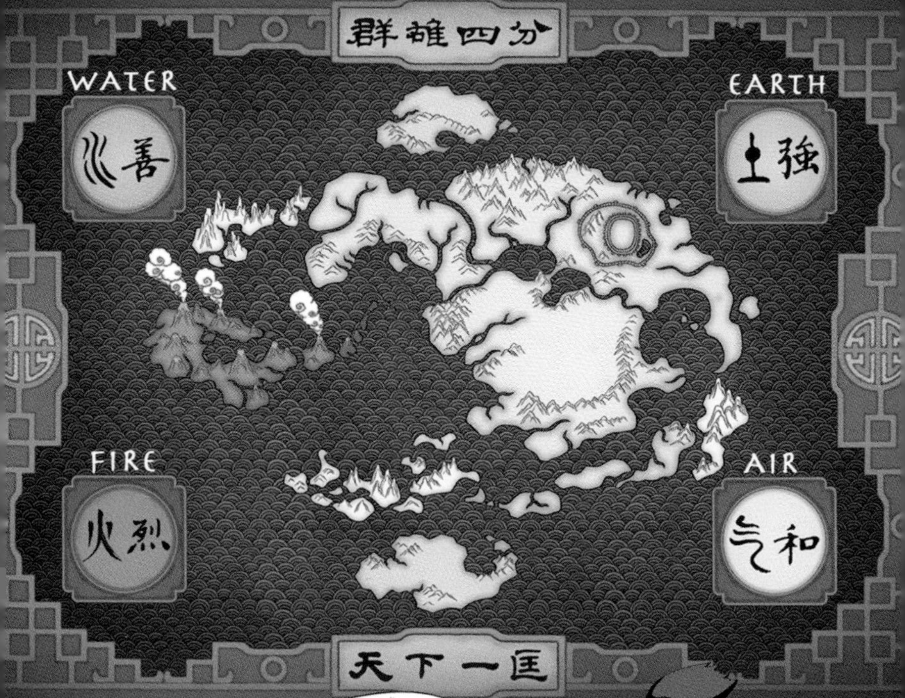
群雄四分
WATER
善
EARTH
強
FIRE
火烈
AIR
和
天下一匡

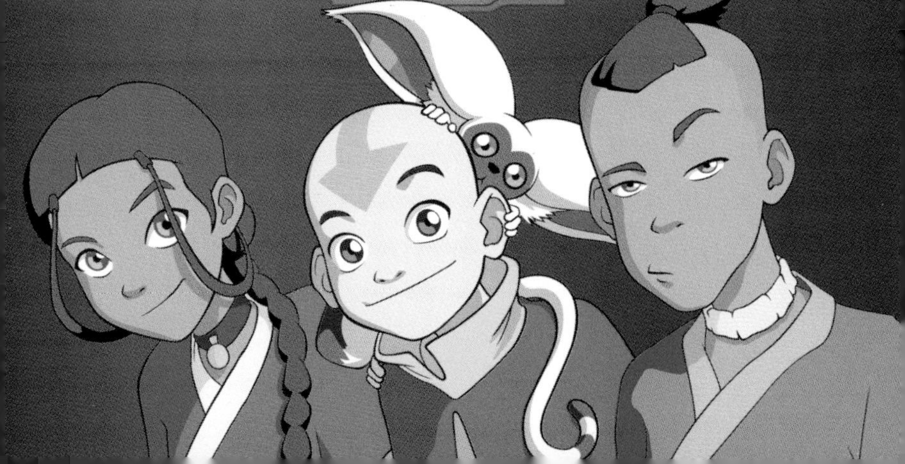

Water Tribes

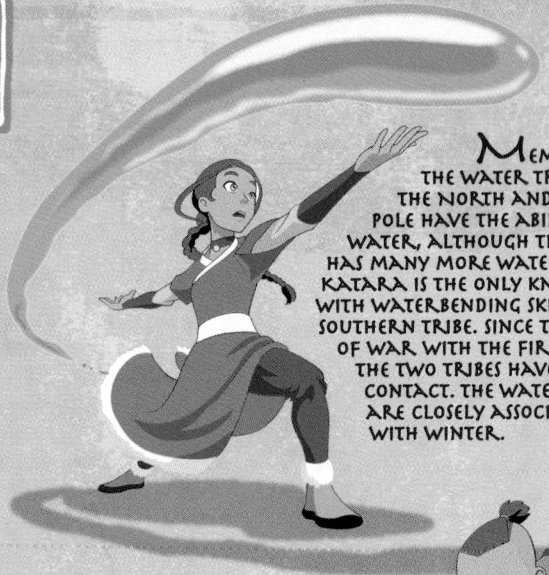

Members of the Water Tribes of the North and South Pole have the ability to bend water, although the North Pole has many more waterbenders. Katara is the only known person with waterbending skill in the Southern Tribe. Since the outbreak of war with the Fire Nation, the two tribes have not had contact. The Water Tribes are closely associated with winter.

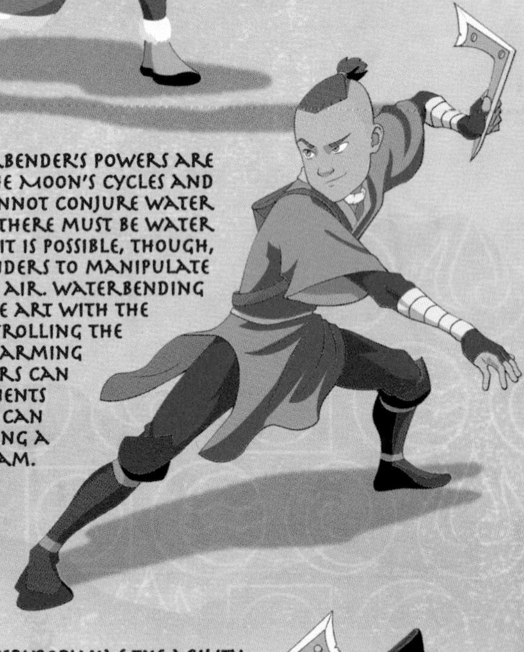

A waterbender's powers are strengthened by the moon's cycles and the rain. They cannot conjure water out of thin air. There must be water around them. It is possible, though, for waterbenders to manipulate moisture in the air. Waterbending is a defensive art with the intention of controlling the opponent, not harming him. Waterbenders can encase their opponents in blocks or they can escape by creating a sheet of steam.

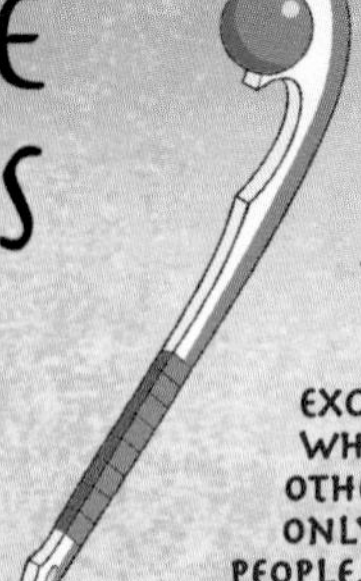

Not everybody has the ability to bend. This is true of all the nations with the one exception being the Air Nomads, who are all airbenders. In the other nations, benders make up only a small percentage of the people. Members of the Water Tribe who do not possess bending skills use boomerangs and staffs as weapons.

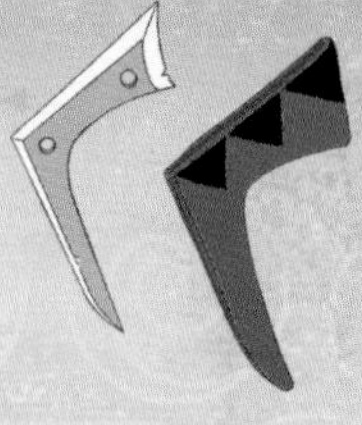

AIR NOMADS

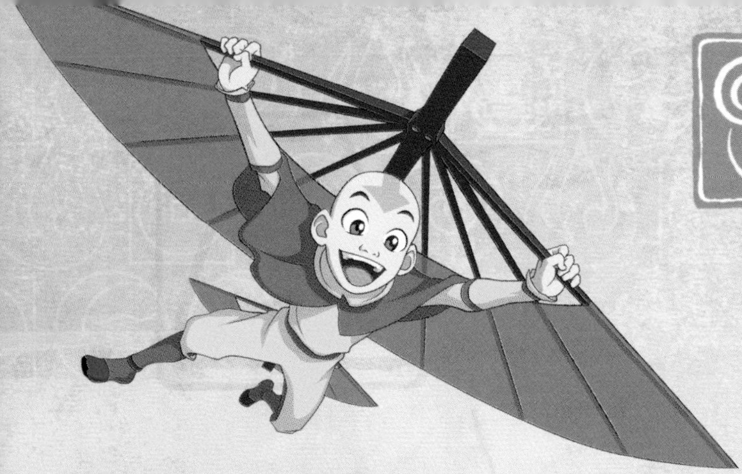

The air nomads travel the world on flying bison, like Appa, but are based at one of four main air temples: North, South, East, or West. Some air nomads live in the temples. The air nomads are a peaceful people and are the most spiritually enlightened of all the nations. They were also the first people to be attacked by the Fire Nation at the beginning of the war. They have not been seen for hundreds of years and are believed to be extinct. The air nomads are closely associated with autumn.

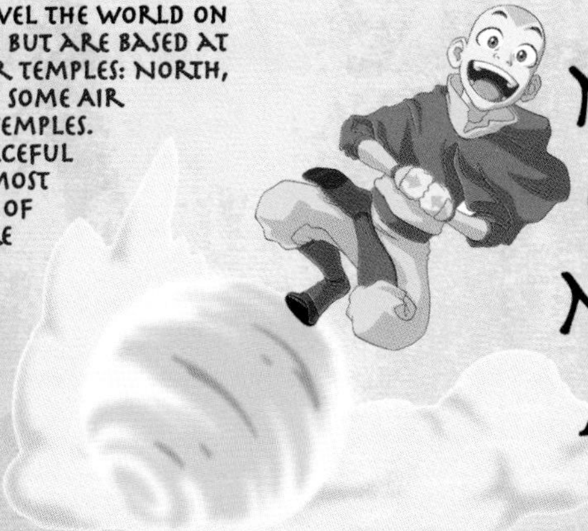

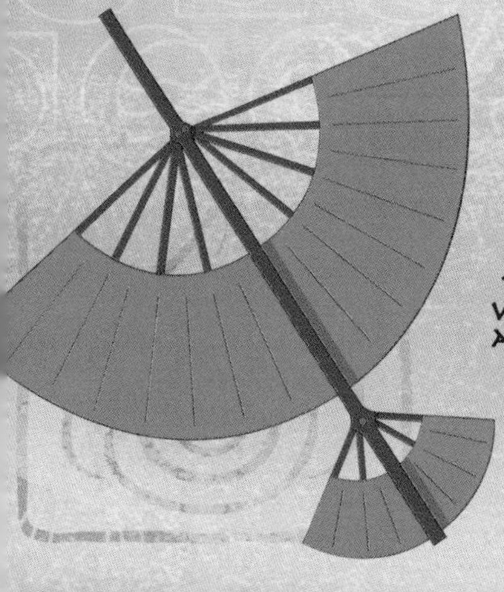

Airbenders cannot fly. They manipulate air currents to enhance their normal movements. As a result, airbenders can jump higher, run faster, and move quicker than other benders. Aang is an extremely skilled airbender. Being the Avatar means that he is the only person in the world who can also bend fire, water, and earth, although his skills are not developed in these areas.

Although airbenders cannot fly, they can ride on air currents using their staffs, which transform into gliders.

FIRE NATION

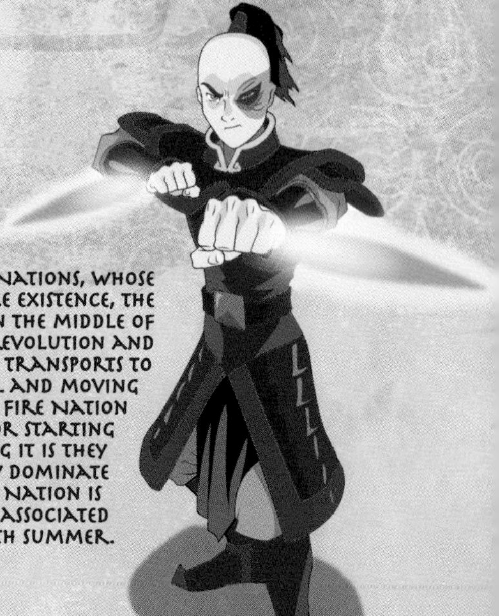

Unlike the air, earth, and water nations, whose people lead a simple existence, the Fire Nation is in the middle of an industrial revolution and has steam-powered transports to help with travel and moving supplies. It is the Fire Nation that is responsible for starting the war, believing it is they who should rightly dominate the world. The Fire Nation is closely associated with summer.

Although firebenders lack defensive powers, they make up for this with a wide variety of offensive moves. A quick jab or kick produces a short-range burst of flame. Whirlwind and spinning kicks produce blazing arcs and rings of fire that explode in all directions with punches creating fireballs. If a number of firebenders combine their power, they can create missiles of flame that can fly over long distances with devastating effects. Although they possess terrifying powers, firebenders have their weaknesses. Their power is influenced by the sun.

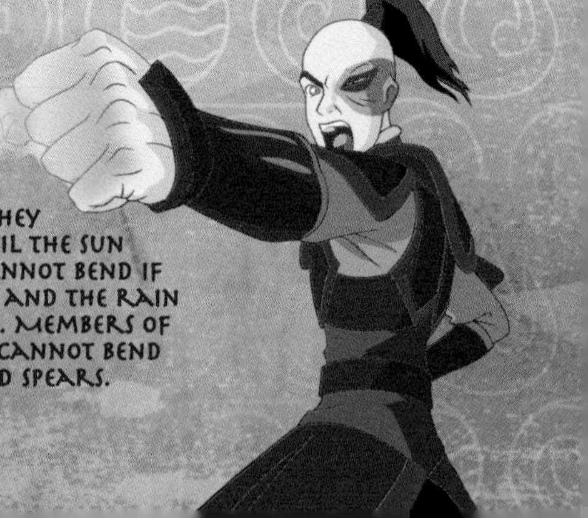

If there is an eclipse, they lose their powers until the sun returns. They also cannot bend if they are underwater, and the rain weakens their powers. Members of the Fire Nation who cannot bend carry swords and spears.

EARTH KINGDOM

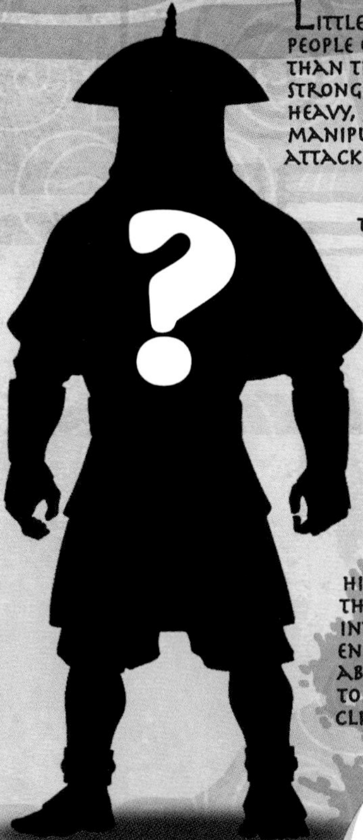

Little is known about the people of this nation other than they are a proud and strong people. Using their heavy, muscular bodies, they manipulate the ground for attack and defense.

They can knock an enemy off his feet by pounding the ground, creating a small earthquake. They can also use the earth to catapult them into the air to avoid attacks and create fissures in the ground to swallow enemies. Other moves include raising stone slabs from the ground for offense and defense, as well as levitating and throwing rocks.

High-level earthbenders have the power to turn the ground into quicksand to trap their enemies. Earthbenders are also able to magnetize their limbs to stone, which allows them to climb walls and cliffs. The Earth Kingdom is closely associated with spring.

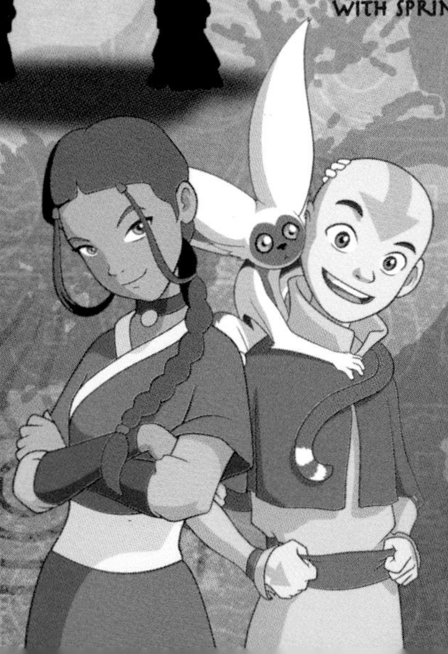

SEE YOU NEXT TIME!

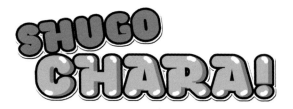

SHUGO CHARA!

PEACH-PIT

Creators of *Dears* and *Rozen Maiden*

Everybody at Seiyo Elementary thinks that stylish and super-cool Amu has it all. But nobody knows the *real* Amu, a shy girl who wishes she had the courage to truly be herself. Changing Amu's life is going to take more than wishes and dreams—it's going to take a little magic! One morning, Amu finds a surprise in her bed: three strange little eggs. Each egg contains a Guardian Character, an angel-like being who can give her the power to be someone new. With the help of her Guardian Characters, Amu is about to discover that her true self is even more amazing than she ever dreamed.

PEACH-PIT
CREATORS OF
DEARS
AND
ROZEN
MAIDEN
SHUGO
CHARA!
1

Special extras in each volume! Read them all!

VISIT WWW.DELREYMANGA.COM TO:
- Read sample pages
- View release date calendars for upcoming volumes
- Sign up for Del Rey's free manga e-newsletter
- Find out the latest about new Del Rey Manga series

DEL REY MANGA デルレイ

The Otaku's Choice

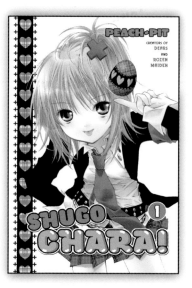

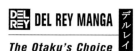

MIKA KAWAMURA

DEMON-FIGHTING RIVALS

Mitsuki and Kakeru are childhood friends—and rivals!

When Mitsuki is attacked by a demon, she and Kakeru discover that they have magical powers. An ancient scroll decrees that they must work together to save the world from a demon invasion. And so their adventure begins!

Special extras in each volume! Read them all!

GHOST HUNT

MANGA BY SHIHO INADA
STORY BY FUYUMI ONO

The decrepit building was condemned long ago, but every time the owners try to tear it down, "accidents" start to happen—people get hurt, sometimes even killed. Mai Taniyama and her classmates have heard the rumors that the creepy old high school is haunted. So, one rainy day they gather to tell ghost stories, hoping to attract one of the suspected spirits. No ghosts materialize, but they do meet Kazuya Shibuya, the handsome young owner of Shibuya Psychic Research, hired to investigate paranormal activity at the school. Also brought to the scene are an exorcist, a Buddhist monk, a woman who can speak with the dead, and an outspoken Shinto priestess. Surely one of them will have the talents to solve this mystery. . . .

Special extras in each volume! Read them all!

DEL REY

VISIT WWW.DELREYMANGA.COM TO:
• Read sample pages
• View release date calendars for upcoming volumes
• Sign up for Del Rey's free manga e-newsletter
• Find out the latest about new Del Rey Manga series